ANNUAL REPORT 2006

Board of Governors of the Federal Reserve System, Federal Deposit Insurance Corporation, National Credit Union Administration, Office of the Comptroller of the Currency, Office of Thrift Supervision, State Liaison Committee

Federal Financial Institutions Examination Council

ANNUAL REPORT 2006

Board of Governors of the Federal Reserve System, Federal Deposit Insurance Corporation, National Credit Union Administration, Office of the Comptroller of the Currency, Office of Thrift Supervision, State Liaison Committee

MEMBERS OF THE COUNCIL

John C. Dugan, *Chairman*
Comptroller of the Currency
Office of the Comptroller of the Currency

Susan Schmidt Bies, *Vice Chairman*
Member, Board of Governors of the
Federal Reserve System

Sheila C. Bair
Chairman
Federal Deposit Insurance Corporation

JoAnn Johnson
Chairman
National Credit Union Administration

John M. Reich
Director
Office of Thrift Supervision

Steven L. Antonakes
Commissioner of Banks
Commonwealth of Massachusetts

LETTER OF TRANSMITTAL

Federal Financial Institutions
　Examination Council
Arlington, VA 22226
March 30, 2007

The President of the Senate
The Speaker of the House of Representatives

Pursuant to the provisions of section 1006(f) of the Financial Institutions Regulatory and Interest Rate Control Act of 1978 (12 USC 3305), I am pleased to submit the 2006 Annual Report of the Federal Financial Institutions Examination Council.

Sincerely,

John C. Dugan
Chairman

TABLE OF CONTENTS

vii Message from the Chairman

1 Overview of the Federal Financial Institutions Examination Council Operations

3 Record of Council Activities

5 State Liaison Report

7 Activities of the Interagency Staff Task Forces

19 The Federal Financial Institution Regulatory Agencies and their Supervised Institutions

23 Assets, Liabilities, and Net Worth of U.S. Commercial Banks, Thrift Institutions, and Credit Unions as of June 30, 2006

24 Income and Expenses of U.S. Commercial Banks, Thrift Institutions, and Credit Unions for Twelve Months Ending June 30, 2006

25 Appendix A: Relevant Statutes

29 Appendix B: 2006 Audit Report

37 Appendix C: Maps of Agency Regions and Districts

43 Appendix D: Organizational Listing of Personnel

MESSAGE FROM THE CHAIRMAN

John C. Dugan

I am pleased to report that the FFIEC continued its high level of performance and productivity throughout 2006. The Council continued to advance its mission of promoting uniformity and consistency in the supervision of financial institutions. The FFIEC also continued to foster communication, cooperation, and coordination among member agencies that make up the Council, its task forces, and the State Liaison Committee, an advisory panel of state financial regulators. In October 2006, the chairman of the State Liaison Committee was added to the membership of the Council.

Details on the 2006 achievements are included later in this report in the Record of Council Activities and Activities of the Interagency Staff Task Forces. I would like to cite here, however, some of the most significant initiatives by the Council, its task forces, and interagency working groups during the year:

- Conducted extensive outreach activities to coordinate and communicate about issues facing the industry in the aftermath of the devastating hurricanes in Louisiana and Mississippi. The agencies initiated a public service campaign to help hurricane victims recover financially and issued joint guidance to examiners outlining supervisory practices to follow in assessing the financial condition of institutions affected by Hurricane Katrina. In addition, the agencies provided guidance to the industry in "Lessons Learned from Hurricane Katrina: Preparing Your Institution for a Catastrophic Event." This booklet relayed financial institutions' experiences and lessons learned in the aftermath of Hurricane Katrina so other institutions could assess their readiness for catastrophic events.

- Revised the 2005 FFIEC's *Bank Secrecy Act/Anti-Money Laundering Examination Manual* to ensure it remains an up-to-date resource for examiners and bankers. In coordination with FinCEN and OFAC, the agencies also conducted four nationwide conference calls with examiners and the industry on the revised manual. More than 10,000 people participated in the calls.

- Updated the FFIEC's Information Security Booklet, part of the FFIEC's IT Examination Handbook. The booklet describes how a financial institution should protect and secure the systems and facilities that process and maintain information. It also includes new or revised material on authentication, risk assessments, monitoring programs, software trustworthiness, "malware," wireless technology, remote access, and trust services.

- Provided data on small business, small farm, and community development lending reported by certain commercial banks and savings institutions, pursuant to the Community Reinvestment Act.

- Provided data for the year 2005 on mortgage lending transactions at 8,848 financial institutions covered by the Home Mortgage Disclosure Act (HMDA) in metropolitan statistical areas (MSAs) throughout the nation. The HMDA data included disclosure statements for each financial institution, aggregate data for each MSA, nationwide summary statistics regarding lending patterns, and the Loan Application Register (modified for borrower privacy) that each institution submitted to its supervisory agency.

- Continued modifications to enhance the FFIEC's Central Data Repository (CDR) system. These enhancements will include the migration of the FFIEC's Uniform Bank Performance Report and the addition of the FDIC's Summary of Deposits data series. The project received four national Information Technology awards in 2006, recognizing its innovative use of eXtensible Business Reporting Language (XBRL) language and collaborative business processes.

- Facilitated discussions on interagency guidance and rules related to banking practices and activities, including:

  a. Frequently Asked Questions (FAQs) to aid in the implementation of the FFIEC's guidance on *Authentication in an Internet Banking Environment* issued in October 2005.

  b. Guidance on Nontraditional Mortgage Products and an addendum to the 2005 Interagency Credit Risk Management Guidance for Home Equity Lending.

  c. Guidance addressing safety and soundness concerns that might arise when financial institutions agree to limit their external auditors' liability.

  d. An updated interagency policy statement on the Allowance for Loan and Lease Losses (ALLL) and a supplement with frequently asked questions about the ALLL. The agencies also developed a training template for examiners on ALLL issues.

  e. An interagency statement alerting financial institutions to revisions to the Uniform Standards for Professional Appraisal Practice (USPAP), issued by the Appraisal Standards Board. Appraisals supporting federally related transactions must adhere to USPAP.

  f. CRA questions and answers to help financial institutions meet their CRA responsibilities.

  g. Updated interagency CRA examination procedures.

- Coordinated joint requests by the agencies for comment on:

  a. Reporting proposals related to regulatory reporting schedules and instructions for collecting data from institutions that have qualified for or are qualifying for the Basel II Advanced Capital Adequacy Framework, or from institutions subject to the agencies' revised market risk capital rules.

  b. An extensive set of proposed Call Report provisions.

- Completed the agencies' solicitation for public comment on regulations that may be outdated, unnecessary, or unduly burdensome on insured depository institutions, pursuant to Section 2222 of the Economic Growth and Regulatory Paperwork Reduction Act of 1996. Some of the recommendations stemming from these comments were incorporated into the Financial Services Regulatory Relief Act of 2006. A final report on the agencies' findings and recommendations will be sent to Congress in early 2007.

- Fostered the continued refinement of protocols for supervisory communications in emergency situations. The protocols are updated quarterly and tested at least annually with key supervisory personnel.

- Delivered training to more than 2,700 state and federal employees, including continuation of the broad-based Supervisory Updates and Emerging Issues conferences and advanced instruction on credit analysis, cash flow construction, fraud, and anti-money laundering.

- Continued enhancements to the speed and accuracy of financial data shared between the agencies.

- Improved access to the Uniform Bank Performance Report by making it public sooner and adding several years of early data.

I am extremely proud of the significant accomplishments that the FFIEC and its task forces achieved in cooperation with the State Liaison Committee in 2006. I am also pleased with our continued communications with other agencies. For example, we consulted with and exchanged information on the application of accounting and auditing standards with the Securities and Exchange Commission, the Financial Accounting Standards Board, the Public Company Accounting Oversight Board, and the American Institute of Certified Public Accountants. We will continue to promote our efforts to work together on an interagency basis to advance our mission of promoting uniformity and consistency in the supervision of our financial institutions.

Overview of the Federal Financial Institutions Examination Council (FFIEC) Operations

The FFIEC was established on March 10, 1979, pursuant to title X of the Financial Institutions Regulatory and Interest Rate Control Act of 1978 (FIRA), Public Law 95-630. The purpose of title X, entitled the Federal Financial Institutions Examination Council Act of 1978, was to create a formal interagency body empowered to prescribe uniform principles, standards, and report forms for the federal examination of financial institutions by the Board of Governors of the Federal Reserve System, the Federal Deposit Insurance Corporation, the National Credit Union Administration, the Office of the Comptroller of the Currency, and the Office of Thrift Supervision and to make recommendations to promote uniformity in the supervision of financial institutions. In accordance with the Financial Services Regulatory Relief Act of 2006, a representative state regulator was added as a member of the FFIEC in October 2006. The Council is also responsible for developing uniform reporting systems for federally supervised financial institutions, their holding companies, and the nonfinancial institution subsidiaries of those institutions and holding companies. It conducts schools for examiners employed by the five member agencies represented on the Council and makes those schools available to employees of state agencies that supervise financial institutions.

The Council was given additional statutory responsibilities by section 340 of the Housing and Community Development Act of 1980, Public Law 96-399. Among these responsibilities are the implementation of a system to facilitate public access to data that depository institutions must disclose under the Home Mortgage Disclosure Act of 1975 (HMDA) and the aggregation of annual HMDA data, by census tract, for each metropolitan statistical area.

Title XI of the Financial Institutions Reform, Recovery, and Enforcement Act of 1989 established the Appraisal Subcommittee within the Council. The functions of the subcommittee are (1) monitoring the requirements, including a code of professional responsibility, established by states for the certification and licensing of individuals who are qualified to perform appraisals in connection with federally related transactions; (2) monitoring the appraisal standards established by the federal financial institutions regulatory agencies and the former Resolution Trust Corporation; (3) maintaining a national registry of appraisers who are certified and licensed by a state and who are also eligible to perform appraisals in federally related transactions; and (4) monitoring the practices, procedures, activities, and organizational structure of the Appraisal Foundation, a nonprofit educational corporation established by the appraisal industry in the United States.

The Council has six members: the Comptroller of the Currency, the Chairman of the Federal Deposit Insurance Corporation, a member of the Board of Governors of the Federal Reserve System appointed by the Chairman of the Board, the Chairman of the Board of the National Credit Union Administration, the Director of the Office of Thrift Supervision, and the Chairman of the State Liaison Committee. To encourage the application of uniform examination principles and standards by the state and federal supervisory authorities, the Council established, in accordance with the requirement of the statute, an advisory State Liaison Committee. To effectively administer projects in all its functional areas, the Council established six interagency staff task forces, each of which includes one senior official from each of the member agencies:

- Consumer Compliance
- Examiner Education
- Information Sharing
- Reports
- Supervision
- Surveillance Systems

The Council also established the Legal Advisory Group, composed of the general or chief counsel of each of the member agencies, to provide support to the Council and staff in the substantive areas of concern; and the Agency Liaison Group, composed of senior officials responsible for coordinating the efforts of their respective agencies' staff members. The task forces and the Legal Advisory Group provide research and analytical papers and proposals on the issues that the Council addresses.

Administration of the Council

The Council holds regular meetings at least twice a year. It holds other meetings whenever called by the Chairman or three or more Council members.

The Council's activities are funded in several ways. Most of the Council's funds are derived from assessments on its five constituent agencies. The Council also receives reimbursement for the services it provides to support preparation of the quarterly Uniform Bank Performance Report. It receives tuition fees from non-agency attendees to cover some of the costs associated with its examiner education program.

In 2006, the Federal Reserve Board provided budget and accounting services to the Council, and the Federal Reserve's Senior Associate Director for Finance served as the Council's controller. The Council is supported by a small, full-time administrative staff in its operations office and in its examiner education program, which are located at the Council's examiner training facility in Arlington, Virginia. Each Council staff member is detailed from one of the five member agencies represented on the Council but is considered an employee of the Council.

RECORD OF COUNCIL ACTIVITIES

The following section is a chronological record of the official actions taken by the FFIEC during 2006 pursuant to the Federal Financial Institutions Examination Council Act of 1978, as amended, and the Home Mortgage Disclosure Act (HMDA).

January 13, 2006

Action. Announced a public service campaign to aid in the financial recovery of victims affected by the Gulf Coast hurricanes.

Explanation. The Council sponsored a series of public service announcements in major U.S. media markets to encourage individuals adversely affected by Hurricanes Katrina and Rita to contact their lenders to discuss options that may be available to assist them.

January 17, 2006

Action. Approved the appointment of Mick Thompson, the Oklahoma State Banking Commissioner, as a member of the FFIEC's State Liaison Committee.

Explanation. In accordance with the FFIEC's Rules of Operations, the Council appoints two of the State Liaison Committee members. The remaining three members are designated by the Conference of State Bank Supervisors, the American Council of State Savings Supervisors, and the National Association of State Credit Union Supervisors.

February 10, 2006

Action. Approved the appointment of Eric McClure, the Commissioner of the Missouri Division of Finance, as a member of the FFIEC's State Liaison Committee.

The Examination Council in Session.

Explanation. In accordance with the FFIEC's Rules of Operations, the Council appoints two of the State Liaison Committee members. The remaining three members are designated by the Conference of State Bank Supervisors, the American Council of State Savings Supervisors, and the National Association of State Credit Union Supervisors.

February 17, 2006

Action. Approved the 2005 annual report of the Council to the Congress.

Explanation. The legislation establishing the Council requires that, not later than April 1 of each year, the Council publish an annual report covering its activities during the preceding year.

March 20, 2006

Action. Approved the issuance of the Council's annual interagency awards.

Explanation. The Council has an interagency awards program that recognizes individuals of the member agencies who have provided outstanding service to the Council on interagency projects and programs during the previous year.

March 27, 2006

Action. Approved the Central Data Repository (CDR) steering committee's request to exercise secondary options and add a new data series to the CDR.

Explanation. The Council was required to approve the exercising of secondary contract options and adding new data series to the CDR. The options will enable the agencies to provide institution and industry Call Report data directly to the public and to process and publish the Uniform Bank Performance Report within the CDR. The Summary of Deposits data series is also being added to the CDR.

March 27, 2006

Action. Approved the appointment of six task force chairs.

Explanation. The chairs for all six standing task forces are approved annually and are drawn from management and staff of the five member agencies.

April 7, 2006

Action. Accepted the annual external audit report.

Explanation. The Council is audited by an outside accounting firm annually. The audit report includes a review of the Council's financial statements as well as a report on internal controls and compliance with government accounting standards.

April 7, 2006

Action. Approved the Task Force on Consumer Compliance's request to develop and publish the Distressed and Underserved Non-Metropolitan Middle-Income geographies listing on the FFIEC website.

Explanation. The data will be presented on the website in a manner that facilitates analysis by users, including bankers, examiners, and the public. Approval by the Council was required since the funds needed to develop the website and publish the information were not originally approved in the 2006 budget.

April 7, 2006

Action. Directed the Task Force on Supervision's Hurricane Katrina working group to memorialize, for the Council, a summary of interagency activities that worked well during the hurricane crises, lessons learned, and recommendations. The Council also approved the development of a document that would be presented to the industry conveying lessons learned and best practices for disasters that are widespread in scope and long-term in duration.

Explanation. The lessons learned were formalized to underscore the importance of coordinating and responding to emerging issues related to the hurricane in a consistent and timely fashion. The lessons-learned booklet for the industry was issued by the FFIEC and Conference of State Bank Supervisors in June 2006.

May 12, 2006

Action. Approved the two-year appointment of Virginia Gibbs as chairperson for the Appraisal Subcommittee.

Explanation. The Council is required by statute to approve the chairperson of the Appraisal Subcommittee.

May 17, 2006

Action. Approved the Memorandum of Understanding (MOU) by and between several member agencies and the Federal Reserve Board regarding the Community Reinvestment Act (CRA) reports.

Explanation. The MOU outlines the responsibilities that the Federal Reserve Board performs related to CRA data that is collected by four of the member agencies from financial institutions that are required to file CRA reports.

July 28, 2006

Action. Approved publication of the revised FFIEC Bank Secrecy Act/Anti-Money Laundering (BSA/AML) Examination Procedures Manual.

Explanation. The BSA/AML Working Group updated the 2005 BSA/AML Manual to ensure it remains an up-to-date resource document for examination staff and the banking industry.

December 13, 2006

Action. Approved the 2007 Council budget.

Explanation. The Council is required to approve the annual budget.

December 13, 2006

Action. Approved the use of the CDR to collect, edit, store and distribute data being considered for Basel II and Market Risk. In addition, the Council approved a Federal Reserve Board primary data collection system as an interim tool until the CDR is ready to be used for the Basel II data collection.

Explanation. Under proposals issued by the federal banking agencies, certain institutions would be required to submit specific data related to Basel II and Market Risk as of March 31, 2008. The CDR is already being used by the agencies to collect and process a series of data related to the quarterly Call Reports filed by insured commercial banks and state-chartered savings banks. In addition, enhancements are in process that will extend the CDR's ability to collect additional data series, such as the Basel II and Market Risk data. In the event the CDR is not ready by the first quarter of 2008, an interim system was approved for data collection.

STATE LIAISON REPORT

The State Liaison Committee consists of five representatives of state agencies that supervise financial institutions. The representatives are appointed for two-year terms. A State Liaison Committee member may have his or her two-year term extended by the appointing organization for an additional, consecutive two-year term. Each year, the State Liaison Committee elects one of its members to serve as chair for twelve months. The Council elects two of the five members. The American Council of State Savings Supervisors, the Conference of State Bank Supervisors, and the National Association of State Credit Union Supervisors designate the other three members. A list of the State Liaison Committee members appears in appendix D of this report.

On October 13, 2006, President George W. Bush signed the Financial Services Regulatory Relief Act of 2006 into law. One of the law's provisions makes the Chairman of the State Liaison Committee a voting member of the Council. Previously, state banking regulators and state credit union supervisors were represented in an observer capacity during monthly meetings of the FFIEC's Task Force on Supervision, the Information Sharing Task Force, the Task Force on Consumer Compliance, and the interagency Bank Secrecy Act/Anti-Money Laundering working group. With the passage of this act, the State Liaison Committee will be appointing state supervisors to represent the state system on all task forces. The State Liaison Committee's involvement with such groups enables state regulators through Conference of State Bank Supervisors, the American Council of State Savings Supervisors, and the National Association of State Credit Union Supervisors to participate in substantive policy discussions on a broad range of important regulatory subjects, reflecting the spirit and intent of Congress in establishing the State Liaison Committee.

The State Liaison Committee looks forward to its enhanced role and continued cooperation of the state and federal regulators.

ACTIVITIES OF THE INTERAGENCY STAFF TASK FORCES

Task Force on Consumer Compliance

The Task Force on Consumer Compliance (TFCC) promotes policy coordination, a common supervisory approach, and uniform enforcement of consumer protection laws and regulations. The task force identifies and analyzes emerging consumer compliance issues and develops proposed policies and procedures to foster consistency among the agencies. Additionally, the task force addresses legislation, regulations, and policies at the state and federal level that may have a bearing on the compliance responsibilities of the five member agencies.

During 2006, the task force used two standing subcommittees to help promote its mission: the Community Reinvestment Act (CRA) Subcommittee and the Home Mortgage Disclosure Act (HMDA)/CRA Data Collection Subcommittee. The TFCC also creates ad hoc working groups to handle particular projects and assignments. The task force meets monthly to address and resolve common issues in compliance supervision. While significant issues or recommendations are referred to the FFIEC for action, the FFIEC has delegated to the task force the authority to make certain decisions and recommendations.

2006 Initiatives

CRA Subcommittee Activities

The Federal Reserve Board, the Office of the Comptroller of the Currency, and the Federal Deposit Insurance Corporation published final questions and answers regarding the substantive changes to the CRA rules that were effective 9/1/05. Among several 2005 changes, the agencies adopted new asset-size thresholds for small and intermediate small banks, including the provision for an annual adjustment to these thresholds based on changes to the consumer price index.

The subcommittee also updated all examination procedures to comply with the 2005 regulatory provision. In addition, the CRA subcommittee continued its review of the 2001 interagency questions and answers and authored updates to the FFIEC web site for these CRA changes and for the data on the distressed and underserved census tracts.

HMDA/CRA Data Collection Subcommittee Activities

After successful implementation of the HMDA Memorandum of Understanding (MOU) in 2005, the subcommittee implemented a CRA MOU between the FFIEC and the Federal Reserve Board's CRA Data Processing unit. The Federal Reserve Board processes HMDA/CRA data on behalf of the FFIEC. The MOU defined the level of service to be provided to the FFIEC. The agencies executed the CRA Data Processing MOU in July 2006.

The subcommittee initiated a CRA efficiency project to identify and implement cost savings in the collection, processing, and reporting of CRA data. The subcommittee also initiated a project to revise the FFIEC's web site. As a result, the agencies will eliminate the Aggregate and Disclosure Report CD-ROM product in 2006, and the reports will be available exclusively on the FFIEC's web site.

Fair Credit Reporting Act (FCRA) Examination Procedures

The TFCC approved newly revised FCRA examination procedures. The procedures incorporate provisions of the FCRA amended by the Fair and Accurate Credit Transactions Act (FACTA). Some of the implementing regulations for the FACTA are not final, so additional procedures will be forthcoming.

Remittances Working Group

The working group looked at edu-

Task Force on Consumer Compliance meeting.

cational resources that address the financial service needs of the growing immigrant community. The group concluded that the development of a multilingual consumer education brochure on remittances is not necessary because brochures exist that assist consumers in understanding their options for remittance services.

Consumer Compliance Hurricane Working Group

The working group provided input to the FFIEC and the Conference of State Bank Supervisors on the "Lessons Learned From Hurricane Katrina: Preparing Your Institution for a Catastrophic Event" document.

Compliance Ratings Definition Working Group

The working group was charged with the task of reviewing the current interagency compliance ratings and possibly redefining the ratings. Work will continue on this project in 2007.

Fair Lending/HMDA Working Group

The Fair Lending/HMDA Working Group was assigned the task of updating the interagency fair lending examination procedures. The working group recommended some changes to the procedures to address pricing disparities. The TFCC decided to postpone revisions to the procedures for one year, in order to gain more experience from the current fair lending examinations. Meanwhile, the agencies will conduct pricing analyses using the current interagency procedures, along with supplemental procedures individually established by each agency. Those analyses will determine whether or how interagency procedures should be revised.

Task Force on Examiner Education

Responsible for overseeing the FFIEC's examiner education program on behalf of the Council, the Task Force on Examiner Education promotes interagency education through timely, cost-efficient, state-of-the-art training programs for agency examiners and staff. The task force develops programs on its own initiative and in response to requests from the Council or other Council task forces. Each fall, it develops a program calendar based on training demand from the five member agencies and state financial institution regulators. The task force also oversees the delivery and evaluation of programs throughout the year. During the past year, over 2,700 regulatory staff members attended training programs. (See the table for details of participation by program and agency.)

Initiatives Addressed in 2006

The Task Force on Examiner Education has continued to ensure that the FFIEC's educational programs meet the needs of agency personnel, are cost–effective, and are widely available. The task force meets monthly with the Examiner Education staff to discuss emerging topics, feedback from each course and conference, and to develop a framework for future conferences and courses. This partnership between the task force and the Examiner Education office continues to result in high quality, well-received training.

The InfoBase architecture implemented in 2001 continues to allow the FFIEC's Examiner Education office to produce training and reference materials that can be delivered on CDs directly to all examiners concurrent with, or shortly after, the issuance of interagency statements, Council courses, or conferences. Updates to the new BSA/AML Examination Manual and the Information Technology Examination Handbook continue to be available to examiners and the industry through its website: www.ffiec.gov.

Facilities

The Council training office and classrooms are located in the Federal Deposit Insurance Corporation Seidman Center in Arlington, Virginia. Offices, classrooms, and lodging facilities are rented from the FDIC. This facility offers convenient access to a 100-seat auditorium and a new auditorium which accommodates

Task Force on Examiner Education meeting.

Student participates in Instructor Training School

250 students classroom-style. Large FFIEC conferences formerly held in hotels around the country are now held in this new auditorium.

Course Catalogue and Schedule

The course catalogue and schedule are available online at www.ffiec.gov/exam/education.htm.

Additionally, a printed copy of the 2007 course catalogue and schedule are available from the Examiner Education Office. To obtain a copy, contact:

2006 FFIEC Training by Agency and Sponsored—Actual, as of December 31, 2006

Event Name	FRB	FRB State Sponsored	FDIC	FDIC State Sponsored	NCUA	OCC	OTS	FCA	FHFB	Other	Total
Advanced Cash Flow Analysis & Concepts	31	15	60	0	16	15	11	0	0	0	148
Advanced Commercial Credit Analysis	29	19	93	20	4	22	9	3	0	0	199
Anti-Money Laundering Workshop	129	55	55	59	13	0	54	0	0	21	386
Asset Management Forum	53	14	37	19	0	29	10	0	1	0	163
Capital Markets Conference	18	16	27	16	10	13	12	0	5	1	118
Capital Markets Specialists Conference	14	13	80	10	17	13	4	9	8	0	168
Cash Flow Construction and Analysis	29	17	66	22	11	18	28	7	0	0	198
Community Financial Institutions Lending Forum	19	14	6	16	8	9	5	0	0	0	77
Financial Crimes Seminar	52	34	74	32	19	0	32	0	1	0	244
Fraud Identification On-line Training	9	0	31	0	0	15	6	1	0	5	67
Fraud Investigations Symposium	3	0	6	0	0	1	1	0	0	0	11
Information Technology Conference	69	13	53	0	7	29	33	12	3	1	220
Instructor Training School	37	2	8	0	5	17	1	5	0	0	75
International Banking Conference	15	2	10	0	0	9	22	0	0	0	58
International Banking School	10	2	2	3	0	4	3	0	0	13	37
International Banking (Self-Study)	6	0	7	0	1	0	19	0	0	47	80
Lead Investigations Specialists Workshop	4	0	3	0	1	4	0	0	0	0	12
Payment Systems Risk Conference	33	13	9	14	12	15	11	1	2	3	113
Real Estate Appraisal Review School	11	17	45	0	6	0	19	1	0	0	99
Real Estate Appraisal Review On-line	0	0	5	0	1	0	1	0	0	0	7
Supervisory Updates & Emerging Issues	80	43	13	23	5	37	27	3	3	0	234
Testifying School	0	2	22	0	2	13	0	0	0	0	39
Grand Total	**651**	**291**	**712**	**234**	**138**	**263**	**308**	**42**	**23**	**91**	**2,753**
Percentage	23.65	10.57	25.86	8.50	5.01	9.55	11.19	1.53	0.84	3.31	100
Combined Agency and Sponsored Percentage	34.22	NA	34.36	NA	5.01	9.55	11.19	1.53	0.84	3.31	100

Jerry LiVigni of the Office of Foreign Asset Control presents at a Money Laundering Workshop.

Karen K. Smith, Manager
FFIEC Examiner Education Office
3501 Fairfax Drive, Room B-3030
Arlington, VA 22226-3550

Phone: (703) 516-5588

Task Force on Information Sharing

The Task Force on Information Sharing promotes the sharing of electronic information among FFIEC agencies in support of the supervision, regulation, and deposit insurance responsibilities of financial institution regulators. The task force provides a forum for FFIEC member agencies to discuss and address issues affecting the quality, consistency, efficiency, and security of interagency information sharing. Significant matters are referred, with recommendations, to the Council for action, and the task force has delegated authority from the Council to take certain actions.

To the extent possible, the agencies build on each other's information databases to minimize duplication of effort and promote consistency. The agencies participate in a program to share, in accordance with agency policy, electronic versions of their reports of examination, inspection reports, and other communications with financial institutions. The agencies also provide each other with access to their organizations' structure, financial, and supervisory information. The task force maintains a "Data Exchange Summary" listing the data files exchanged among FFIEC agencies.

Task Force on Information Sharing meeting.

Task force members consist of representatives from FFIEC agencies. Monthly meetings are held to address and resolve issues related to information sharing. In addition, the task force receives demonstrations and reports on agency, financial industry, and other FFIEC initiatives pertaining to technology development. The task force has established two working groups to address technology-development issues and interagency reconciliation of financial institution structure data.

Initiatives Addressed in 2006

Technology Issues

The chief initiative of the task force is to identify and implement technologies to make the sharing of interagency data more efficient and to accommodate changes in agency databases and technologies. The task force's Technology Working Group meets monthly to develop technological solutions to common data-sharing issues among the agencies. The working group coordinates the automated transfer of data files among the agencies and suggests better and more efficient ways to share financial and supervisory data. The working group also maintains a Task Scope Matrix to identify and provide status reports on all outstanding work group projects.

High-speed T1 communication lines linking the Federal Deposit Insurance Corporation, the Federal Reserve Board, and the Office of the Comptroller of the Currency have eliminated the use of magnetic tapes or disks for sharing electronic data among these agencies. Further research is being conducted to ensure efficiency of data utilization through the reduction of volume and duplication of efforts. New technologies are being implemented in improving data sharing.

In 2006, the group continued to work on long-term projects related to the FRB's planned new bulk data transfer, National Information Center (NIC) Architecture Redesign Initiative, and changes to NIC tables to implement the Structure Processing Application, and the OCC's planned retirement of its mainframe. Completed projects include sharing new information to assess risk-related deposit insurance premiums and archiving historical data from the collaborative web site. Efforts continue to establish an automated mechanism to secure data transfers between the Federal Reserve Board and the National Credit Union Association.

Structure Data Reconciliation

The task force's Structure Data Reconciliation Working Group continues to reconcile structure data about financial institutions regulated by FFIEC agencies to ensure that the information the agencies report is consistent and accurate. The working group's quarterly reconcilements have greatly resolved data discrepancies among the agencies.

Collaborative Web Site

The Information Sharing Task Force and the Technology Working Group use an FDIC-sponsored collaborative web site to share information among the FFIEC agencies. The web site is used to disseminate documents and other critical materials pertaining to interagency information exchanges.

Task Force on Reports

The law establishing the Council and defining its functions requires the Council to develop uniform reporting systems for federally supervised financial institutions and their holding companies and subsidiaries. To meet this objective, the Council established the Task Force on Reports. The task force helps to develop interagency uniformity in the reporting of periodic information that is needed for effective supervision and other public policy purposes. As a consequence, the task force is concerned with issues such as the development and interpretation of reporting instructions, including responding to inquiries about the instructions from reporting institutions and the public; the application of accounting standards to specific transactions; the development and application of processing standards; the monitoring of data quality; and the assessment of reporting burden. In addition, the task force works with other organizations, including the Securities and Exchange Commission, the Financial Accounting Standards Board, and the American Institute of Certified Public Accountants. The task force is also responsible for any special projects related to these subjects that the Council may assign. To help the task force carry out its responsibilities, working groups are organized as needed to handle specialized or technical accounting, reporting, instructional, and processing matters.

Initiatives Addressed in 2006

Central Data Repository (CDR)

During 2006, the Federal Deposit Insurance Corporation, the Federal Reserve Board, and the Office of the Comptroller of the Currency (the agencies) devoted significant staff resources to enhancing the CDR for processing the quarterly Consolidated Reports of Condition and Income (Call Reports) filed by insured commercial banks and state-chartered savings banks. The CDR steering committee continued to coordinate

Central Data Repository Steering Committee meeting.

the agencies' work on this project and used several focus groups to collaborate and communicate with contractors and targeted stakeholder communities. The agencies allocated staff resources to ongoing CDR aintenance and several system enhancements including extensibility (to add the Summary of Deposits, Basel II, and Market Risk data series to the CDR) and secondary options (the Call Report facsimile web site, an online analytical processing tool, and the Uniform Bank Performance Report).

The CDR Help Desk handled a lower volume of calls in 2006 from respondents, most of them related to user maintenance issues. The agencies continued to see improvement in the quality of data received, and bankers continued to submit their data slightly earlier in the reporting cycle than prior to implementation of the CDR.

During 2006, the CDR project team focused on resolving system issues, suggesting contract modifications to improve functionality, training agency users, and developing plans for implementing the functionality for the secondary options. The CDR team wrote a detailed overall project plan, which integrated the work for individual tasks; developed a 2-year operating plan for 2006 and 2007 to address enhancements, secondary options, and adding new data series; and developed a 5-year strategic plan to address expansion of the CDR through 2010.

The project team began in mid-2006 to focus on requirements gathering for extending the CDR. This extensibility work will continue through 2007. The extensibility requirements were gathered in two parts: requirements for adding new data series and requirements for enhancing the staff's ability to manage the metadata data used to create the taxonomies.

The CDR project received four national information technology awards in 2006 for its innovative use of the XBRL standard and collaborative business processes.

Reporting Requirements for the Call Report

In January 2006, banks were notified that the implementation of proposed revisions to the Call Report that had been issued for public comment in August 2005 would be phased in over the two-year period from March 2006 through March 2008 and that some of the proposed reporting changes had been modified. The task force took this approach because many of the comments on the Call Report revisions addressed the proposed March 2006 effective date and indicated that a longer implementation period would be needed to make the systems changes required to support several of the proposed revisions. In February 2006, the task force approved, and the Federal Reserve Board, the Office of the Comptroller of the Currency, and the Federal Deposit Insurance Corporation published, a final Paperwork Reduction Act (PRA) Federal Register notice on these Call Report revisions. The U.S. Office of Management and Budget (OMB) approved the revisions and the implementation schedule in March 2006.

Under the schedule adopted by the task force, the Call Report revisions that took effect March 31, 2006, included eliminating or limiting the applicability of existing data items for estimated uninsured deposits, asset-backed securities held as investments, income from nontrading derivatives, and bankers acceptances; adding items for life insurance assets, types of credit derivatives, and remaining maturities of credit derivatives; and revising the reporting of income from international operations. As of September 30, 2006, items pertaining to Federal Home Loan Bank advances and other borrowings, nonaccrual assets, certain secured borrowings, and residential mortgage banking activities were added or revised. On that date, a revised officer signature and attestation requirement, which began to apply to each bank's chief financial officer, also took effect.

Effective March 31, 2007, revisions will be made to the reporting of lease financing receivables; income from annuity sales, investment banking, securities brokerage, and securities underwriting; and trading revenues by type of exposure. On that date, new items will also be added for residential mortgage banking revenues and net gains and losses on certain credit derivatives. In addition, beginning March 31, 2007, all banks with $300 million or more in assets and certain smaller banks will report additional information on their real estate construction loans and their nonfarm nonresidential real estate loans. Other banks with less than $300 million in assets will begin to provide this additional loan detail beginning March 31, 2008.

Effective April 1, 2006, the Federal Deposit Insurance Corporation increased the deposit insurance limit for certain retirement plan deposit accounts from $100,000 to $250,000 as required by the Federal Deposit Insurance Reform Act of 2005 (Reform Act), enacted in February 2006. In response to this increase in insurance coverage, the task force revised the reporting of information in the Call Report and the Report of Assets and Liabilities for U.S. Branches and Agencies of Foreign Banks (FFIEC 002) on the number and amount of deposit accounts within and in excess of the deposit insurance limits. The existing items on accounts subject to the previous uniform limit of $100,000 were supplemented by new items for retirement deposit accounts to which the $250,000 limit applies. The task force approved, and in May and July 2006, the Federal Reserve Board, the Office of the Comptroller of the Currency, and the Federal Deposit Insurance Corporation published Federal Register notices concerning the retirement deposit account revisions to the Call Report, which took effect in June 2006 subject to transition guidance. The task force also approved, and in June and August 2006 the

Federal Reserve Board, on behalf of the three agencies, published Federal Register notices describing comparable revisions to the FFIEC 002 report. The retirement deposit account changes to this report took effect in September 2006 subject to transition guidance.

In October 2006, the task force approved, and the four banking agencies jointly published, an initial PRA Federal Register notice requesting comment on proposed revisions to the Call Report and the Thrift Financial Report (TFR) involving data for deposit insurance assessment purposes and large denomination Individual Retirement Account and Keogh Plan time deposits. The proposal also included the addition of new Call Report data items pertaining to residential mortgages with negative amortization features as well as assets and liabilities accounted for at fair value under new fair value option accounting and measurement standards. These proposed revisions are scheduled to take effect March 31, 2007, but with a transition period until March 31, 2008, for the assessment-related changes. The comment period for these proposed revisions ended January 2, 2007. After considering the comments received, the task force approved certain modifications to the proposal and agreed to move forward with the modified reporting changes on March 31, 2007, and 2008. The banking agencies published a final PRA notice concerning these reporting revisions in February 2007 and subsequently notified institutions about the revisions, which OMB must approve before they become final.

Section 601 of the Financial Services Regulatory Relief Act of 2006 (Relief Act), which became effective on October 13, 2006, eliminated the requirement that an institution include a separate report with its Call Report and TFR each quarter on any extensions of credit the institution has made to its executive officers since the date of its last report. As a consequence, the "Special Report" on loans to executive officers, which previously had been included with the Call Report and TFR to enable institutions to report these extensions of credit, was discontinued as of December 31, 2006.

The task force conducted monthly interagency conference calls during 2006 to discuss Call Report instructional matters and related accounting issues to reach uniform interagency positions on these issues.

Other Activities

In July 2006, the task force approved, and the Federal Reserve Board, the Office of the Comptroller of the Currency, and the Federal Deposit Insurance Corporation jointly published, an initial PRA Federal Register notice requesting comment on a proposal to significantly streamline the reporting requirements for the FFIEC 030, Foreign Branch Report of Condition. As proposed, foreign branches with less than $50 million in assets would be exempt from reporting and foreign branches with between $50 million and $250 million in assets would file an abbreviated report containing five items (the FFIEC 030S). For larger branches, five items from the existing FFIEC 030 report would be eliminated. The agencies received no comments on the proposal. The task force approved and the agencies published a final PRA Federal Register notice concerning the proposed streamlining in October 2006. OMB approved these reporting changes in November 2006. The revised reporting requirements, which took effect at year-end 2006, significantly reduced or eliminated the burden of the FFIEC 030 report for approximately two-thirds of foreign branches of U.S. banks.

In September 2006, the task force approved proposed regulatory reporting requirements for the agencies' use in evaluating and monitoring the levels and components of each reporting entity's risk-based capital requirements, the reasonableness of its calculations, and the adequacy of its capital under the agencies' proposed Advanced Capital Adequacy Framework (known as Basel II) and their proposed market risk rules, particularly in relation to the entity's risks. The four banking agencies' joint initial PRA Federal Register notices for these two sets of proposed reporting requirements were published for comment on the same date (September 25, 2006) and for the same comment periods as the agencies' notices of proposed rulemaking for these two risk-based capital proposals. As developed by an interagency Data Collection Group of subject matter experts, the reporting proposals include:

- A set of 22 proposed reporting schedules and their related instructions, designated the FFIEC 101 data series, that would be used to collect data from banks, savings associations, and bank holding companies that have qualified for or are qualifying for the Basel II framework; and

- One proposed reporting schedule and its related instructions, designated the FFIEC 102 data series, that would be used to collect data from banks, savings associations, and bank holding companies subject to the agencies' revised market risk capital rules.

As proposed, reported data would not be publicly available except for two of the schedules and a portion of a third schedule in the FFIEC 101 data series. However, these data would be available for an individual reporting entity only for periods after it has completed its parallel run. On December 13, 2006, the Council approved the use of the CDR as the collection system for the FFIEC 101 and FFIEC 102 data series and the use of the Federal Reserve Board's Statistics and Reserves (STAR) system as a potential interim collection system.

In March 2006, the task force completed the implementation of revisions to the FFIEC 009, Country Exposure Report, that are providing additional detail on U.S. banks' exposure to country risk, transfer risk, and foreign exchange risk while eliminating certain previously collected data items from the report. The revisions have harmonized U.S. data with data on cross-border exposures collected by other countries and disseminated by the Bank for International Settlements.

OMB approved a three-year extension of the authority for the Federal Reserve Board, the Office of the Comptroller of the Currency, and the Federal Deposit Insurance Corporation to collect the FFIEC 009 and the supplemental FFIEC 009a, Country Exposure Information Report, in April 2006. OMB also approved a three-year extension of the agencies authority to collect the FFIEC 019, Country Exposure Report for U.S. Branches and Agencies of Foreign Banks, in September 2006. Both of these approvals followed the agencies' publication of initial and final PRA Federal Register notices.

Task Force on Supervision

The Task Force on Supervision coordinates and oversees matters relating to safety-and-soundness supervision and examination of depository institutions. It provides a forum for the member agencies to promote quality, consistency, and effectiveness in examination and supervisory practices and to reduce unnecessary regulatory burden. While significant issues are referred, with recommendations, to the Council for action, the Council has delegated to the task force the authority to make certain decisions and recommendations, provided all task force members agree. Meetings are held regularly to address and resolve common supervisory issues. To facilitate communication and coordination with the Council's State Liaison Committee, representatives of the State Liaison Committee attended task force meetings on an advisory basis during 2006. The task force has also established and maintains supervisory communication protocols to be used in emergencies. These protocols are periodically tested through table-top exercises with task force members and key supervisory personnel.

The task force has three standing subcommittees:

- The Capital Subcommittee serves as a forum for senior policy staff members to discuss various initiatives pertaining to the agencies' regulatory capital standards.

- The Information Technology (IT) Subcommittee serves as a forum to address information systems and technology issues as they relate to financial institutions. The IT Subcommittee oversees and administers the FFIEC's Technology Service Provider (TSP) and Shared Application Software Reveiw (SASR) programs. Through the FFIEC'S Multi-Regional Data Processing Servicer (MDPS) program, the agencies conduct joint information technology examinations of the largest technology service providers and other entities that provide critical banking services. The SASR program provides a mechanism for the agencies to review and share information on mission-critical software applications, such as loans, deposits, general ledger systems, and other critical software tools that are used by a large number of financial institutions. These reviews can help the agencies identify potential systemic risks and provide examiners with information that can reduce time and resources needed to examine the software at each of the user financial institutions.

- The Bank Secrecy Act/Anti-Money Laundering (BSA/AML) Working Group seeks to enhance coordination of BSA/AML training, guidance, and policy. The coordination includes continuing communication between federal and state banking agencies and the Financial Crimes Enforcement Network. The BSA/AML Working Group builds on existing efforts and works to strengthen the activities that are already being pursued by other formal and informal interagency groups providing oversight of various BSA/AML matters. BSA/AML training, guidance, and policy includes: (1) procedures and resource materials for examina-

Task Force on Supervision meeting.

tion purposes; (2) joint examiner training related to the Manual; (3) outreach to the banking industry on BSA/AML policy matters; and (4) other issues related to consistency of BSA/AML supervision. The BSA/AML Working Group published a revised Manual in July of 2006 that further clarified supervisory expectations and incorporated regulatory changes since the Manual's inception. The revisions drew upon feedback from the banking industry and examination staff.

The task force also establishes ad hoc working groups to handle individual projects and assignments, as needed.

Initiatives Addressed in 2006

Information Technology

Financial institutions' significant use of information technology services, whether generated internally or obtained from third-party service providers, contributes to their operational risk environment in general and their data security risk in particular. The Task Force's Information Technology (IT) Subcommittee serves as a focal point for coordinating many of the agencies' supervisory activities in these areas. A major effort of the subcommittee and agencies is maintaining the FFIEC IT Examination Handbook, which was first published in 1996. This handbook was replaced by a series of twelve topical booklets addressing issues such as business continuity planning, information security, and electronic banking. In 2006, the group published an updated Information Security Booklet.

The Information Technology Subcommittee, in conjunction with the Task Force on Examiner Education, sponsors an annual IT conference for the agencies' examination staff to explore emerging risks and industry best practices. This subcommittee also periodically hosts a MDPS examiner conference to discuss risk trends and supervisory strategies applicable to large technology service providers and an IT examiner symposium that develops guidance on emerging technologies that are expected to affect the banking industry. A MDPS conference was held in March 2006.

Capital Standards

Although each of the four federal banking agencies has its own capital regulations, the task force's standing Capital Subcommittee and several of its working groups often coordinate efforts among the agencies to promote joint issuance of capital rules and related interpretive guidance, thereby minimizing interagency differences and reducing the potential burden on the banking industry. A major focus of the federal banking agencies has been the development of the proposed Basel II framework. An interagency proposal (NPR) was issued for public comment in October 2006.

The agencies also have worked together to consider ways to (1) modernize the risk-based capital rules for non-Basel II banks to ensure that the framework remains relevant and (2) minimize potentially material differences in capital requirements that may arise between banks that adopt Basel II and those banks that remain under the existing rules. This effort culminated in an interagency NPR, also known as Basel IA, that was released in December of 2006 to solicit comments on potential revisions to the existing risk-based capital framework.

The two NPRs, Basel II and Basel IA, were published with overlapping comment periods to give the industry an opportunity to comment on both at the same time to assess the interaction of the two proposals. The comment period for both NPRs ended March 26, 2007.

Other Supervisory Initiatives

Throughout the year, the task force discusses and responds to emerging supervisory issues and risks. During 2006, the task force oversaw the development and issuance of the following interagency supervisory policy statement and advisories.

- A revised Interagency Policy Statement on the Allowance for Loan and Lease Losses and supplemental Frequently Asked Questions was issued in December 2006 and a final case study and common training template for examiner training on the allowance were completed in early 2006.

- Interagency Guidance on Non-Traditional Mortgages which addresses loan terms and underwriting standards, portfolio risk-management practices, and consumer protection issues that could arise with these products was issued in September 2006.

- Interagency Commercial Real Estate Risk Management Guidance which addresses the sound risk management practices for concentrations in commercial real estate lending. The guidance reinforces existing guidelines for real estate lending and safety and soundness. It provides criteria for identifying institutions with commercial real estate loan concentrations that may warrant greater supervisory scrutiny.

- Interagency Advisory on External Auditors/Limitation of Liability addresses clauses in external auditor engagement letters that raise supervisory concerns. The guidance was released in early 2006.

- Lessons Learned from Hurricane Katrina booklet that conveyed lessons learned and best practices for disasters that are wide-spread in scope and long-term in duration.

Task Force on Surveillance Systems

The Task Force on Surveillance Systems oversees the development and implementation of uniform interagency surveillance and monitoring systems. It provides a forum for the member agencies to discuss best practices to be used in those systems and to consider the development of new financial analysis tools. The task force's principal objective has been to develop and produce the Uniform Bank Performance Report (UBPR). UBPRs present financial statistics and peer group comparisons of individual banks for current and historical periods. These reports are important tools for completing supervisory evaluations of a bank's condition and performance, as well as for planning onsite examinations. The banking agencies also use the data from these reports in their automated monitoring systems to identify potential or emerging problems in insured banks.

UBPRs are produced for each commercial bank and insured savings bank in the United States that is supervised by the Federal Reserve Board, the Federal Deposit Insurance Corporation, or the Office of the Comptroller of the Currency. UBPR data are also available to all state bank supervisors. While the UBPR is principally designed to meet the examination and surveillance needs of the federal and state banking agencies, the task force also makes UBPRs available to banks and the public through a public web site; www.ffiec.gov.

Initiatives Addressed in 2006

Early UBPR Data Delivered

The task force implemented a new process that allows UBPR data for individual banks to be published shortly after the underlying Call Report has been validated in the FFIEC Central Data Repository. For many banks this change meant that UBPR information became available 15 days prior to the Call Report filing deadline.

Task Force on Surveillance Systems meeting.

Early Peer Group Statistics Delivered

After a thorough review of the underlying information, the task force decided to again shorten the delivery time for peer group statistics and percentile rankings. Peer group and percentile ranking data is now available within 5 days of the filing date for the call report form.

Historical UBPR Data Now Available

The task force decided to extend the range of UBPR data available on the website back to 1995. Individual bank data as well as peer group statistics and percentile rankings are available for almost 10 years. This newly available information reflects current UBPR data and peer group definitions. The FFIEC plans to retain 1995 as the earliest date and expand the database going forward.

New UBPR Data Added

The task force added a complete page of information about Concentrations of Credit to the Uniform Bank Performance Report. A detailed comparison of several loan categories is available along with peer group average and percentile ranking data.

User's Guide (Guide) for the UBPR

The Guide was updated to incorporate new samples of pages and associated data. The March 31, 2006 version of the guide is available online at www.ffiec.gov.

Enhancements to the UBPR

In 2007, the task force planned several enhancements to the UBPR that will take advantage of new and existing Call Report data. Additionally, the custom peer search engine may be expanded to permit several additional search criteria. Advance notice of changes will be provided on http://www.ffiec.gov/UBPR.htm. The task force is also participating with the Task Force on Reports and the Central Data Repository (CDR) Steering Committee in implementing a move of Uniform Bank Performance Report processing to the CDR.

Information Available on the UBPR Web Site

UBPR Availability

To provide broad public access to information about the financial condition of insured banks, the task force publishes a final quarterly version of the UBPR for each institution, typically within twenty to twenty-five days of the Call Report due date. Additionally, early UBPR data is typically available 15 days before the Call Report filing date. Bankers and the general public may access these reports on the FFIEC web site at no charge. In addition to publishing current reports, the task force regularly refreshes all historic UBPR data on the web site.

Other UBPR Reports

Several web-based statistical reports supporting UBPR analysis are also updated on the web site. These reports (1) summarize the performance of each of the UBPR's peer groups (determined by size, location, and business line), (2) detail the distribution of UBPR performance ratios for banks in each of these peer groups, (3) list the individual banks included in each peer group, and (4) compare a bank to the performance of a user-defined customer peer group.

Custom Peer Group Tool

The Custom Peer allows bankers, bank supervisors, and the general public to create custom peer groups based on financial and geographical criteria and to display all UBPR pages with peer group statistics and percentile rankings derived from a custom peer group.

Please visit http://www.ffiec.gov/UBPR.htm for additional information about the UBPR, including distribution schedules, descriptions of pending changes, and instructions on using online UBPR tools. Standardized UBPR quarterly data on cartridge is also available for $400. Information on ordering items may be obtained by calling (703) 516-5732, sending an e-mail message to JSmullen@fdic.gov, or writing the Council at:

Federal Financial Institutions
 Examination Council
3501 Fairfax Drive, Room D8073a
Arlington, VA 22226-3550

THE FEDERAL FINANCIAL INSTITUTION REGULATORY AGENCIES AND THEIR SUPERVISED INSTITUTIONS

The five federal regulatory agencies represented on the Council have primary federal supervisory jurisdiction over 18,558 domestically chartered banks, thrift institutions, and credit unions. On June 30, 2006, these financial institutions held total assets of more than $12.3 trillion. The Board of Governors of the Federal Reserve System and the Office of Thrift Supervision also have primary federal supervisory responsibility for commercial bank holding companies and for savings and loan holding companies, respectively.

Three banking agencies on the Council have authority to oversee the operations of U.S. branches and agencies of foreign banks. The International Banking Act of 1978 (IBA) authorizes the Office of the Comptroller of the Currency to license federal branches and agencies of foreign banks and permits U.S. branches that accept only wholesale deposits to apply for insurance with the Federal Deposit Insurance Corporation. According to the Federal Deposit Insurance Corporation Improvement Act of 1991 (FDICIA), foreign banks that wish to operate insured entities in the United States and accept retail deposits must organize under separate U.S. charters. Existing insured retail branches may continue to operate as branches. The IBA also subjects those U.S. offices of foreign banks to many provisions of the Federal Reserve Act and the Bank Holding Company Act. The IBA gives primary examining authority to the Office of the Comptroller of the Currency, the Federal Deposit Insurnace Corporation, and various state authorities for the offices within their jurisdictions and gives the Federal Reserve Board residual examining authority over all U.S. banking operations of foreign banks.

Board of Governors of the Federal Reserve System

The Federal Reserve Board was established in 1913. It is headed by a seven-member Board of Governors, each member of which is appointed by the President, with the advice and consent of the Senate, for a fourteen-year term. Subject to confirmation by the Senate, the President selects two Board members to serve four-year terms as Chairman and Vice Chairman. The Federal Reserve Board's activities that are most relevant to the work of the Council are the following:

- examining, supervising, and regulating state member banks (that is, state-chartered banks that are members of the Federal Reserve System); bank holding companies; Edge Act and agreement corporations; and, in conjunction with the licensing authorities, the U.S. offices of foreign banks;

- developing and issuing regulations, policies, and guidance applicable to organizations within the Federal Reserve Board's supervisory oversight authority; and

- approving or denying applications for mergers, acquisitions, and changes in control by state member banks and bank holding companies, applications for foreign operations of member banks and Edge Act and agreement corporations, and applications by foreign banks to establish or acquire U.S. banks and to establish U.S. branches, agencies, or representative offices.

Other supervisory and regulatory responsibilities of the Federal Reserve Board include regulating margin requirements on securities transactions, implementing certain statutes that protect consumers in credit and deposit transactions, monitoring compliance with other statutes (for example, the money-laundering provisions of the Bank Secrecy Act), and regulating transactions between banking affiliates.

Policy decisions are implemented by the Federal Reserve Board and the twelve Federal Reserve Banks, each of which has operational responsibility within a specific geographical area. The twelve Reserve Bank Districts are headquartered in Boston, New York, Philadelphia, Cleveland, Richmond, Atlanta, Chicago, St. Louis, Minneapolis, Kansas City, Dallas, and San Francisco. Each Reserve Bank has a president and other officers. Among other responsibilities, a Reserve Bank employs a staff of bank examiners who examine state member banks and Edge Act and agreement corporations, inspect bank holding companies, and examine the offices of foreign banks located within the Reserve Bank's District.

National banks, which must be members of the Federal Reserve, are chartered, regulated, and supervised by the Office of the Comptroller of the Currency. State-chartered banks may apply to and be accepted for membership in the Federal Reserve System, after which they are subject to the supervision and regulation of the Federal Reserve Board. Insured state-chartered banks that are not members of the Federal Reserve System are regulated and supervised by the FDIC. The Federal Reserve Board has overall responsibility for foreign banking operations, including both U.S. banks operating abroad and foreign banks operating branches in the United States.

The Federal Reserve Board covers the expenses of its operations with revenue it generates principally from assessments on the twelve Federal Reserve Banks.

Federal Deposit Insurance Corporation

Congress created the Federal Deposit Insurance Corporation in 1933 with a mission to insure bank deposits and reduce the economic disruptions caused by bank failures. Management of the Federal Deposit Insurance Corporation is vested in a five-member Board of Directors. Three of the directors are directly appointed by the President, with the advice and consent of the Senate, for six-year terms. One of the three directors is designated by the President as Chairman for a term of five years, and another is designated as Vice Chairman. The other two Board members are the Comptroller of the Currency and the Director of the Office of Thrift Supervision. No more than three board members may be of the same political party.

The Federal Deposit Insurance Corporation's supervisory activities are conducted by the Division of Supervision and Consumer Protection. The division is organized into six regional offices and two area offices. The regional offices are located in Atlanta, Chicago, Dallas, Kansas City, New York, and San Francisco. The two area offices are located in Boston (reports to New York) and Memphis (reports to Dallas). In addition to the regional and area offices, the Federal Deposit Insurance Corporation maintains fifty-two field territory offices for risk management and thirty-two field territory offices for compliance, with dedicated examiners assigned to the six largest financial institutions. Bank liquidations are handled by the Division of Resolutions and Receiverships.

On February 8, 2006, the President signed the Federal Deposit Insurance Reform Act of 2005 (the Reform Act) into law. The Federal Deposit Insurance Reform Conforming Amendments Act of 2005 was signed into law on February 15, 2006, and contains necessary technical and conforming changes to implement deposit insurance requirements. The Reform Act provided for significant changes to the deposit insurance system. The Bank Insurance Fund (BIF) and Savings Association Insurance Fund (SAIF) were merged into the Deposit Insurance Fund (DIF) on March 31, 2006. The DIF now insures deposits at all commercial banks and savings institutions. The general coverage limit remains at $100,000 but, effective April 1, 2006, the coverage limit for certain retirement accounts was raised to $250,000. Coverage for these accounts along with the general deposit insurance coverage limit are indexed to inflation with potential increases (in $10,000 increments) every five years beginning January 1, 2011, if the Federal Deposit Insurance Corporation and National Credit Union Administration determine that increases are warranted. Effective January 1, 2007, the Federal Deposit Insurance Corporation was given the ability to manage the reserve ratio within a range of 1.15 percent to 1.50 percent of estimated insured deposits with certain restrictions. The Federal Deposit Insurance Corporation may now charge a risk-based assessment to all insured institutions regardless of the level of the reserve ratio. Beginning in 2007, assessment rates will range between five and forty-three cents for every $100 of assessable deposits. Each institution's rate will depend on the degree of risk that it poses to the DIF. The Reform Act granted assessment credits to many institutions to recognize past contributions to the fund. Institutions that have credits may use them to offset deposit insurance assessments, subject to some statutory restrictions.

Any depository institution that receives deposits may be insured by the Federal Deposit Insurance Corporation after application to and examination and approval by the Federal Deposit Insurance Corporation. After considering the (1) applicant's financial history and condition, (2) adequacy of the capital structure, (3) future earnings prospects, (4) general character of the management, (5) risk presented to the insurance fund, (6) convenience and needs of the community to be served, and (7) consistency of corporate powers, the Federal Deposit Insurance Corporation may approve or deny an application for insurance. The FDICIA expanded the Federal Deposit Insurance Corporation's approval authority to include national banks, all state-chartered banks that are members of the Federal Reserve System, and federal and state-chartered savings associations.

The Federal Deposit Insurance Corporation has primary federal regulatory and supervisory authority over insured state-chartered banks that are not members of the Federal Reserve System, and it has the authority to examine for insurance purposes any insured financial institution, either directly or in cooperation with state or other federal supervisory authorities. The FDICIA gives the Federal Deposit Insurance Corporation backup enforcement authority over all insured institutions; that is, the Federal Deopsit Insurance Corporation can recommend that the appropriate federal agency take action against an insured institution and may do so itself if deemed necessary.

In protecting insured deposits, the Federal Deposit Insurance Corporation is charged with resolving the problems of insured depository institutions at the least possible cost to the deposit insurance fund. In carrying out this responsibility the Federal Deposit Insurance Corporation engages in several activities, including paying off deposits, arranging the purchase of assets and assumption of liabilities of failed institutions, effecting insured deposit transfers between institutions, creating and operating temporary bridge banks until a resolution can be accomplished, and using its conservatorship powers.

National Credit Union Administration

The National Credit Union Administration, established by an act of Congress in 1934, is the agency that supervises the nation's federal credit union system. A three-member bipartisan board appointed by the President for six-year terms manages the National Credit Union Administration. The President also selects a member to serve as Chair of the board.

The main responsibilities of the National Credit Union Administration are the following:

- charter, examine, and supervise more than 5,200 federal credit unions nationwide;
- administer the National Credit Union Share Insurance Fund (NCUSIF), which insures member share accounts in more than 8,400 U.S. federal and state-chartered credit unions; and
- manage the Central Liquidity Facility, a central bank for credit unions, which provides liquidity to the credit union system.

The National Credit Union Administration also has statutory authority to examine and supervise NCUSIF-insured, state-chartered credit unions in coordination with state agencies.

The National Credit Union Administration has five regional offices across the United States that administer its responsibility to charter and supervise credit unions. Its examiners conduct on-site examinations and supervision of each federal credit union and selected state-chartered credit unions. The National Credit Union Administration is funded by the credit unions it regulates and insures.

Office of the Comptroller of the Currency

The Office of the Comptroller of the Currency is the oldest federal bank regulatory agency, established as a bureau of the Treasury Department by the National Currency Act of 1863. It is headed by the Comptroller of the Currency, who is appointed to a five-year term by the President with the advice and consent of the Senate. The Comptroller also serves as a Director of the Federal Deposit Insurance Corporation and as a Director of the Neighborhood Reinvestment Corporation.

The Office of the Comptroller of the Currency was created by Congress to charter national banks, to oversee a nationwide system of banking institutions, and to assure that national banks are safe and sound, competitive and profitable, and capable of serving in the best possible manner the banking needs of their customers. The Office of the Comptroller of the Currency regulates and supervises approximately 1,830 national banks and trust companies and 50 federal branches of foreign banks in the United States, accounting for about 67 percent of the total assets of all U.S. commercial banks and branches of foreign banks.

The Office of the Comptroller of the Currency seeks to ensure a banking system in which national banks soundly manage their risks, comply with applicable laws, compete effectively with other providers of financial services, offer products and services that meet the needs of customers, and provide fair access to financial services and fair treatment of their customers. The Office of the Comptroller of the Currency's mission-critical programs include:

- Chartering national banks and issuing interpretations related to permissible banking activities.
- Establishing and communicating regulations, policies, and operating guidance applicable to national banks.
- Supervising the national banking system through on-site examinations, off-site monitoring, systemic risk analyses, and appropriate enforcement activities.

To meet its objectives, the Office of the Comptroller of the Currency maintains a nationwide staff of bank examiners and other professional and support personnel. Headquartered in Washington, D.C., the Office of the Comptroller of the Currency has four district offices in Chicago, Dallas, Denver and New York. In addition, the Office of the Comptroller of the Currency maintains a network of 52 field offices and 25 satellite locations in cities throughout the United States, as well as resident examiner teams in the 22 largest national banking companies and an examining office in London, England.

The Comptroller receives advice on policy and operational issues from an Executive Committee, comprised of senior agency officials who lead major business units.

The Office of the Comptroller of the Currency is funded primarily by semiannual assessments on national banks, interest revenue from its investment in U.S. Treasury securities, and other fees. The Office of the Comptroller of the Currency does not receive congressional appropriations for any of its operations.

Office of Thrift Supervision

The Office of Thrift Supervision was established as a bureau of the U. S. Department of the Treasury in 1989. The Office of Thrift Supervision charters and is the primary regulator for all federal savings associations, and shares joint responsibility with state authorities for supervision of all state savings associations. The Office of Thrift Supervision is also the primary regulator for all savings and loan holding companies, and has been affirmed by the European Union to be the consolidated, coordinating regulator for specific holding companies conducting operations in Europe.

The mission of the Office of Thrift Supervision is to perform the following tasks:

- effectively and efficiently supervise savings associations;
- supervise savings and loan hold-

ing company enterprises to assess corporate-wide risk and capital adequacy;

- maintain the safety, soundness, and viability of the thrift institution industry; and
- encourage a competitive industry to meet America's housing, consumer credit, and financial services needs and to provide access to financial services for all Americans.

The Office of Thrift Supervision carries out its mission by (1) adopting regulations governing the thrift institution industry, (2) examining and supervising savings associations and their affiliates, (3) taking appropriate action to enforce compliance with federal laws and regulations, and (4) acting on applications to charter or acquire a savings association. The Office of Thrift Supervision also has the authority to regulate, examine, supervise, and take enforcement action against savings and loan holding companies and other affiliates, as well as entities that provide services to savings associations.

The Office of Thrift Supervision is headed by a Director appointed by the President, with the advice and consent of the Senate, to serve a five-year term. The Director determines policy for the Office of Thrift Supervision and makes final decisions on regulations governing the industry as a whole and on measures affecting individual institutions. The Director also serves as a Director of the Federal Deposit Insurance Corporation and as a Director of the Neighborhood Reinvestment Corporation.

The agency conducts its operations from its headquarters in Washington, D.C., and four regional offices located in Jersey City, New Jersey (Northeast Region); Atlanta, Georgia (Southeast Region); Dallas, Texas (Midwest Region); and Daly City, California (West Region).

The Office of Thrift Supervision uses no congressional appropriations to fund any of its operations. It draws its revenues primarily through fees and assessments levied on the institutions it regulates.

ASSETS, LIABILITIES, AND NET WORTH of U.S. Commercial Banks, Thrift Institutions and Credit Unions as of June 30, 2006[1]

Billions of dollars

Item	Total	U.S. Commercial Banks[2]			U.S. Branches and Agencies of Foreign Banks[5]	Thrift Institutions			Credit Unions[3]	
						OTS-Regulated[4]		Other FDIC-Insured Savings Banks		
		National	State Member	State Non-Member		Federal Charter	State Charter		Federal Charter	State Charter
Total assets	**13,662**	**6,414**	**1,358**	**1,782**	**1,490**	**1,572**	**14**	**335**	**389**	**308**
Total loans and receivables (net)	7,820	3,541	833	1,187	393	1,169	9	214	259	215
Loans secured by real estate[6]	4,640	1,854	504	804	23	1,031	9	182	125	108
Consumer loans[7]	1,147	577	78	145	0	92	0	14	135	106
Commercial and industrial loans	1,371	730	177	188	204	51	0	17	2	2
All other loans and lease receivables[8]	741	422	84	64	166	2	0	3	0	0
LESS: Allowance for possible loan and lease losses	78	42	10	14	0	7	0	2	2	2
Federal funds sold and securities purchased under agreements to resell	711	417	20	48	193	23	0	7	3	1
Cash and due from depository institutions[9]	593	257	78	61	64	27	1	8	55	42
Securities and other obligations[10]	2,214	1,007	281	354	156	237	4	82	56	37
U.S. government obligations[11]	628	103	66	139	24	151	3	63	49	30
Obligations of state and local governments[12]	135	64	20	41	0	7	0	3	0	0
Other securities	1,451	840	195	174	132	79	1	16	7	7
Other assets[13]	2,324	1191	146	132	684	116	1	24	17	13
Total liabilities	**12,414**	**5,790**	**1,219**	**1,588**	**1,490**	**1,401**	**12**	**296**	**344**	**274**
Total deposits and shares[14]	8,834	4,085	971	1,325	737	875	11	236	332	262
Federal funds purchased and securities sold under agreements to repurchase	1,094	562	92	94	246	82	0	15	3	0
Other borrowings[15]	1,581	652	110	142	210	408	1	42	7	9
Other liabilities[16]	904	491	45	27	297	36	0	3	3	2
Net worth[17]	**1,248**	**625**	**138**	**194**	**0**	**171**	**2**	**39**	**45**	**35**
Memorandum: Number of institutions reporting	17,559	1,777	897	4,795	251	768	86	445	5,308	3,232

Footnotes to Tables

1. The table covers institutions, including those in Puerto Rico and U.S. territories and possessions, insured by the Federal Deposit Insurance Corporation or National Credit Union Savings Insurance Fund. All branches and agencies of foreign banks in the United States, but excluding any in Puerto Rico and U.S. territories and possessions, are covered whether or not insured. Excludes Edge Act and agreement corporations that are not subsidiaries of U.S. commercial banks.

2. Reflects fully consolidated statements of FDIC-insured U.S. banks—including their foreign branches, foreign subsidiaries, branches in Puerto Rico and U.S. territories and possessions, and FDIC insured banks in Puerto Rico and U.S. territories and possessions. Excludes bank holding companies.

3. Data are for federally insured natural person credit unions only.

4. Data for thrift institutions regulated by the OTS are unconsolidated except for operating and finance subsidiaries.

5. These institutions are not required to file reports of income.

6. Includes loans secured by residential property, commercial property, farmland (including improvements) and unimproved land; and construction loans secured by real estate.

7. Includes loans, except those secured by real estate, to individuals for household, family, and other personal expenditures including both installment and single payment loans. Net of unearned income on installment loans.

8. Includes loans to financial institutions, for purchasing or carrying securities, to finance agricultural production and other loans to farmers (except those secured by real estate), to states and political subdivisions and public authorities, and miscellaneous types of loans.

9. Includes vault cash, cash items in process of collection, and balances with U.S. and foreign banks and other depository institutions (including demand and time deposits and certificates of deposit for all categories of institutions).

Notes continue on the next page

INCOME AND EXPENSES of U.S. Commercial Banks and Thrift Institutions for Twelve Months Ending June 30, 2006[1]
Billions of dollars

		U.S. Commercial Banks[2]			Thrift Institutions			Credit Unions[3]	
					OTS-Regulated[4]		Other FDIC-Insured Savings Banks		
Item	Total	National	State Member	State Non-Member	Federal Charter	State Charter		Federal Charter	State Charter
Operating income	858	460	101	129	106	1	17	25	19
Interest and fees on loans	476	230	52	82	71	1	11	16	13
Other interest and dividend income	142	81	17	19	14	0	4	4	3
All other operating income	240	149	32	27	21	0	2	5	4
Operating expenses	649	346	75	94	83	0	13	21	17
Salaries and benefits	162	87	20	25	15	0	4	6	5
Interest on deposits and shares	179	89	20	30	22	0	5	7	6
Interest on other borrowed money	96	55	9	9	21	0	1	0	0
Provision for loan and lease losses	32	19	3	4	3	0	0	1	1
All other operating expenses	180	95	23	26	22	0	3	6	5
Net operating income	**208**	**114**	**26**	**35**	**23**	**0**	**4**	**3**	**2**
Securities gains and losses	4	0	0	0	4	0	0	0	0
Income taxes	67	37	8	11	10	0	1	0	0
Net income	**145**	**77**	**18**	**24**	**17**	**0**	**3**	**3**	**2**
Memorandum: Number of institutions reporting	17,308	1,777	897	4,795	768	86	445	5,308	3,232

10. Includes government and corporate securities, including mortgage-backed securities and obligations of states and political subdivisions and of U.S. government agencies and corporations.

11. U.S. Treasury securities and securities of, and loans to, U.S. government agencies and corporations.

12. Securities issued by states and political subdivisions and public authorities, except for savings and loan associations and U.S. branches and agencies of foreign banks that do not report these securities separately. Loans to states and political subdivisions and public authorities are included in "All other loans and lease receivables."

13. Customers' liabilities on acceptances, real property owned, various accrual accounts, and miscellaneous assets. For U.S. branches and agencies of foreign banks, also includes net due from head office and other related institutions. For SAIF-insured institutions, also includes equity investment in service corporation subsidiaries.

14. Includes demand, savings, and time deposits, (including certificates of deposit at commercial banks, U.S. branches and agencies of foreign banks, and savings banks), credit balances at U.S. agencies of foreign banks and share balances at savings and loan associations and credit unions (including certificates of deposit, NOW accounts, and share draft accounts). For U.S. commercial banks, includes deposits in foreign offices, branches in U.S. territories and possessions, and Edge Act and Agreement corporation subsidiaries.

15. Includes interest-bearing demand notes issued to the U.S. Treasury, borrowing from Federal Reserve Banks and Federal Home Loan Banks, subordinated debt, limited life preferred stock, and other nondeposit borrowing.

16. Includes depository institutions' own mortgage borrowing, liability for capitalized leases, liability on acceptances executed, various accrual accounts, and miscellaneous liabilities. For U.S. branches and agencies of foreign banks, also includes net owed to head office and other related institutions.

17. Includes capital stock, surplus, capital reserves, and undivided profits.

NOTE: Data are rounded to nearest billion. Consequently, some information may not reconcile precisely. Additionally, balances less than $500 million will show as zero.

APPENDIX A: RELEVANT STATUTES

Federal Financial Institutions Examination Council Act

12 U.S.C. § 3301. Declaration of purpose

It is the purpose of this chapter to establish a Financial Institutions Examination Council which shall prescribe uniform principles and standards for the Federal examination of financial institutions by the Office of the Comptroller of the Currency, the Federal Deposit Insurance Corporation, the Board of Governors of the Federal Reserve System, the Federal Home Loan Bank Board, and the National Credit Union Administration and make recommendations to promote uniformity in the supervision of these financial institutions. The Council's actions shall be designed to promote consistency in such examination and to insure progressive and vigilant supervision.

12 U.S.C. § 3302. Definitions

As used in this chapter—

(1) the term "Federal financial institutions regulatory agencies" means the Office of the Comptroller of the Currency, the Board of Governors of the Federal Reserve System, the Federal Deposit Insurance Corporation, the Office of Thrift Supervision, and the National Credit Union Administration;

(2) the term "Council" means the Financial Institutions Examination Council; and

(3) the term "financial institution" means a commercial bank, a savings bank, a trust company, a savings association, a building and loan association, a homestead association, a cooperative bank, or a credit union.

12 U.S.C. § 3303. Financial Institutions Examination Council

(a) Establishment; composition

There is established the Financial Institutions Examination Council which shall consist of—

(1) the Comptroller of the Currency,

(2) the Chairman of the Board of Directors of the Federal Deposit Insurance Corporation,

(3) a Governor of the Board of Governors of the Federal Reserve System designated by the Chairman of the Board,

(4) the Director, Office of Thrift Supervision,

(5) the Chairman of the National Credit Union Administration Board; and

(6) the Chairman of the State Liaison Committee

(b) Chairmanship

The members of the Council shall select the first chairman of the Council. Thereafter the chairmanship shall rotate among the members of the Council.

(c) Term of office

The term of the Chairman of the Council shall be two years.

(d) Designation of officers and employees

The members of the Council may, from time to time, designate other officers or employees of their respective agencies to carry out their duties on the Council.

(e) Compensation and expenses

Each member of the Council shall serve without additional compensation but shall be entitled to reasonable expenses incurred while carrying out his official duties as such a member.

12 U.S.C. § 3304. Costs and expenses of Council

One-fifth of the costs and expenses of the Council, including the salaries of its employees, shall be paid by each of the Federal financial institutions regulatory agencies. Annual assessments for such share shall be levied by the Council based upon its projected budget for the year, and additional assessments may be made during the year, if necessary.

12 U.S.C. § 3305. Functions of Council

(a) Establishment of principles and standards

The Council shall establish uniform principles and standards and report forms for the examination of financial institutions which shall be applied by the Federal financial institutions regulatory agencies.

(b) Making recommendations regarding supervisory matters and adequacy of supervisory tools

(1) The Council shall make recommendations for uniformity in other supervisory matters, such as, but not limited to, classifying loans subject to country risk, identifying financial institutions in need of special supervisory attention, and evaluating the soundness of large loans that are shared by two or more financial institutions. In addition, the Council shall make recommendations regarding the adequacy of supervisory tools for determining the impact of holding company operations on the financial institutions within the holding company and shall consider the

ability of supervisory agencies to discover possible fraud or questionable and illegal payments and practices which might occur in the operation of financial institutions or their holding companies.

(2) When a recommendation of the Council is found unacceptable by one or more of the applicable Federal financial institutions regulatory agencies, the agency or agencies shall submit to the Council, within a time period specified by the Council, a written statement of the reasons the recommendation is unacceptable.

(c) Development of uniform reporting system

The Council shall develop uniform reporting systems for federally supervised financial institutions, their holding companies, and non-financial institution subsidiaries of such institutions or holding companies. The authority to develop uniform reporting systems shall not restrict or amend the requirements of section 78l(i) of Title 15.

(d) Conducting schools for examiners and assistant examiners

The Council shall conduct schools for examiners and assistant examiners employed by the Federal financial institutions regulatory agencies. Such schools shall be open to enrollment by employees of State financial institutions supervisory agencies and employees of the Federal Housing Finance Board under conditions specified by the Council.

(e) Affect on Federal regulatory agency research and development of new financial institutions supervisory agencies

Nothing in this chapter shall be construed to limit or discourage Federal regulatory agency research and development of new financial institutions supervisory methods and tools, nor to preclude the field testing of any innovation devised by any Federal regulatory agency.

(f) Annual report

Not later than April 1 of each year, the Council shall prepare an annual report covering its activities during the preceding year.

(g) Flood insurance

The Council shall consult with and assist the Federal entities for lending regulation, as such term is defined in section 4121(a) of Title 42, in developing and coordinating uniform standards and requirements for use by regulated lending institutions under the national flood insurance program.

12 U.S.C. § 3306. State liaison

To encourage the application of uniform examination principles and standards by State and Federal supervisory agencies, the Council shall establish a liaison committee composed of five representatives of State agencies which supervise financial institutions which shall meet at least twice a year with the Council. Members of the liaison committee shall receive a reasonable allowance for necessary expenses incurred in attending meetings.

Members of the Liaison Committee shall elect a chairperson from among the members serving on the committee.

12 U.S.C. § 3307. Administration

(a) Authority of Chairman of Council

The Chairman of the Council is authorized to carry out and to delegate the authority to carry out the internal administration of the Council, including the appointment and supervision of employees and the distribution of business among members, employees, and administrative units.

(b) Use of personnel, services, and facilities of Federal financial institutions regulatory agencies, Federal Reserve banks, and Federal Home Loan Banks

In addition to any other authority conferred upon it by this chapter, in carrying out its functions under this chapter, the Council may utilize, with their consent and to the extent practical, the personnel, services, and facilities of the Federal financial institutions regulatory agencies, Federal Reserve banks, and Federal Home Loan Banks, with or without reimbursement therefor.

(c) Compensation, authority, and duties of officers and employees; experts and consultants

In addition, the Council may—

(1) subject to the provisions of Title 5 relating to the competitive service, classification, and General Schedule pay rates, appoint and fix the compensation of such officers and employees as are necessary to carry out the provisions of this chapter, and to prescribe the authority and duties of such officers and employees; and

(2) obtain the services of such experts and consultants as are necessary to carry out the provisions of this chapter.

12 U.S.C. § 3308. Access to books, accounts, records, etc., by Council

For the purpose of carrying out this chapter, the Council shall have access to all books, accounts, records, reports, files, memorandums, papers, things, and property belonging to or in use by Federal financial institutions regulatory agencies, including reports of examination of financial institutions or their holding companies from whatever source, together with workpapers and correspondence files related to such reports, whether or not a part of the report, and all without any deletions.

12 U.S.C. § 3309. Risk management training

(a) Seminars

The Council shall develop and administer training seminars in risk management for its employees and the employees of insured financial institutions.

(b) Study of risk management training program

Not later than end of the 1-year period beginning on August 9, 1989, the Council shall—

(1) conduct a study on the feasibility and appropriateness of establishing a formalized risk management training program designed to lead to the certification of Risk Management Analysts; and

(2) report to the Congress the results of such study.

12 U.S.C. § 3310. Establishment of Appraisal Subcommittee

There shall be within the Council a subcommittee to be known as the "Appraisal Subcommittee," which shall consist of the designees of the heads of the Federal financial institutions regulatory agencies. Each such designee shall be a person who has demonstrated knowledge and competence concerning the appraisal profession.

12 U.S.C. § 3311. Required review of regulations

(a) In general

Not less frequently than once every 10 years, the Council and each appropriate Federal banking agency represented on the Council shall conduct a review of all regulations prescribed by the Council or by any such appropriate Federal banking agency, respectively, in order to identify outdated or otherwise unnecessary regulatory requirements imposed on insured depository institutions.

(b) Process

In conducting the review under subsection (a) of this section, the Council or the appropriate Federal banking agency shall—

(1) categorize the regulations described in subsection (a) of this section by type (such as consumer regulations, safety and soundness regulations, or such other designations as determined by the Council, or the appropriate Federal banking agency); and

(2) at regular intervals, provide notice and solicit public comment on a particular category or categories of regulations, requesting commentators to identify areas of the regulations that are outdated, unnecessary, or unduly burdensome.

(c) Complete review

The Council or the appropriate Federal banking agency shall ensure that the notice and comment period described in subsection (b)(2) of this section is conducted with respect to all regulations described in subsection (a) of this section not less frequently than once every 10 years.

(d) Regulatory response

The Council or the appropriate Federal banking agency shall—

(1) publish in the Federal Register a summary of the comments received under this section, identifying significant issues raised and providing comment on such issues; and

(2) eliminate unnecessary regulations to the extent that such action is appropriate.

(e) Report to Congress

Not later than 30 days after carrying out subsection (d)(1) of this section, the Council shall submit to the Congress a report, which shall include—

(1) a summary of any significant issues raised by public comments received by the Council and the appropriate Federal banking agencies under this section and the relative merits of such issues; and

(2) an analysis of whether the appropriate Federal banking agency involved is able to address the regulatory burdens associated with such issues by regulation, or whether such burdens must be addressed by legislative action.

Excerpts from Statute Governing Appraisal Subcommittee

12 U.S.C. § 3332. Functions of Appraisal Subcommittee

(a) In general

The Appraisal Subcommittee shall—

(1) monitor the requirements established by States for the certification and licensing of individuals who are qualified to perform appraisals in connection with federally related transactions, including a code of professional responsibility;

(2) monitor the requirements established by the Federal financial institutions regulatory agencies and the Resolution Trust Corporation with respect to—

(A) appraisal standards for federally related transactions under their jurisdiction, and

(B) determinations as to which federally related transactions under their jurisdiction require the services of a State certified appraiser and which require the services of a State licensed appraiser;

(3) maintain a national registry of State certified and licensed appraisers who are eligible to perform appraisals in federally related transactions; and

(4) Omitted.

(b) Monitoring and reviewing Foundation

The Appraisal Subcommittee shall monitor and review the practices, procedures, activities, and organizational structure of the Appraisal Foundation.

12 U.S.C. § 3333. Chairperson of Appraisal Subcommittee; term of Chairperson; meetings

(a) Chairperson

The Council shall select the Chairperson of the subcommittee. The term of the Chairperson shall be two years.

Excerpts from Home Mortgage Disclosure Act

12 U.S.C. § 2801. Congressional findings and declaration of purpose

(a) Findings of Congress

The Congress finds that some depository institutions have sometimes contributed to the decline of certain geographic areas by their failure pursuant to their chartering responsibilities to provide adequate home financing to qualified applicants on reasonable terms and conditions.

(b) Purpose of chapter

The purpose of this chapter is to provide the citizens and public officials of the United States with sufficient information to enable them to determine whether depository institutions are filling their obligations to serve the housing needs of the communities and neighborhoods in which they are located and to assist public officials in their determination of the distribution of public sector investments in a manner designed to improve the private investment environment.

(c) Construction of chapter

Nothing in this chapter is intended to, nor shall it be construed to, encourage unsound lending practices or the allocation of credit.

12 U.S.C. § 2803. Maintenance of records and public disclosure

(f) Data disclosure system; operation, etc.

The Federal Financial Institutions Examination Council, in consultation with the Secretary, shall implement a system to facilitate access to data required to be disclosed under this section. Such system shall include arrangements for a central depository of data in each primary metropolitan statistical area, metropolitan statistical area, or consolidated metropolitan statistical area that is not comprised of designated primary metropolitan statistical areas. Disclosure statements shall be made available to the public for inspection and copying at such central depository of data for all depository institutions which are required to disclose information under this section (or which are exempted pursuant to section 2805(b) of this title) and which have a home office or branch office within such primary metropolitan statistical area, metropolitan statistical area, or consolidated metropolitan statistical area that is not comprised of designated primary metropolitan statistical areas.

12 U.S.C. § 2809. Compilation of aggregate data

(a) Commencement; scope of data and tables

Beginning with data for calendar year 1980, the Federal Financial Institutions Examination Council shall compile each year, for each primary metropolitan statistical area, metropolitan statistical area, or consolidated metropolitan statistical area that is not comprised of designated primary metropolitan statistical areas, aggregate data by census tract for all depository institutions which are required to disclose data under section 2803 of this title or which are exempt pursuant to section 2805(b) of this title. The Council shall also produce tables indicating, for each primary metropolitan statistical area, metropolitan statistical area, or consolidated metropolitan statistical area that is not comprised of designated primary metropolitan statistical areas, aggregate lending patterns for various categories of census tracts grouped according to location, age of housing stock, income level, and racial characteristics.

(b) Staff and data processing resources

The Board shall provide staff and data processing resources to the Council to enable it to carry out the provisions of subsection (a) of this section.

(c) Availability to public

The data and tables required pursuant to subsection (a) of this section shall be made available to the public no later than December 31 of the year following the calendar year on which the data is based.

APPENDIX B: 2006 AUDIT REPORT

KPMG LLP
2001 M Street, NW
Washington, DC 20036

Independent Auditors' Report

To the Federal Financial Institutions Examination Council:

We have audited the accompanying balance sheets of the Federal Financial Institutions Examination Council (the Council) as of December 31, 2006 and 2005, and the related statements of revenues and expenses and changes in cumulative results of operations, and cash flows (hereinafter referred to as "financial statements") for the years then ended. These financial statements are the responsibility of the Council's management. Our responsibility is to express an opinion on these financial statements based on our audits.

We conducted our audits in accordance with auditing standards generally accepted in the United States of America and the standards applicable to financial audits contained in *Government Auditing Standards*, issued by the Comptroller General of the United States. Those standards require that we plan and perform the audits to obtain reasonable assurance about whether the financial statements are free of material misstatement. An audit includes consideration of internal control over financial reporting as a basis for designing audit procedures that are appropriate in the circumstances, but not for the purpose of expressing an opinion on the effectiveness of the Council's internal control over financial reporting. Accordingly, we express no such opinion. An audit also includes examining, on a test basis, evidence supporting the amounts and disclosures in the financial statements, assessing the accounting principles used and significant estimates made by management, as well as evaluating the overall financial statement presentation. We believe that our audits provide a reasonable basis for our opinion.

In our opinion, the financial statements referred to above present fairly, in all material respects, the financial position of the Federal Financial Institutions Examination Council, as of December 31, 2006 and 2005, and the results of its operations, and its cash flows, for the years then ended, in conformity with U.S. generally accepted accounting principles.

In accordance with *Government Auditing Standards*, we have also issued our reports dated March 7, 2007, on our consideration of the Council's internal control over financial reporting and our tests of its compliance with certain provisions of laws, regulations, contracts, and other matters. The purpose of those reports is to describe the scope of our testing of internal control over financial reporting and compliance and the results of that testing, and not to provide an opinion on the internal control over financial reporting or on compliance. Those reports are an integral part of an audit performed in accordance with *Government Auditing Standards* and should be read in conjunction with this report in assessing the results of our audits.

KPMG LLP

March 7, 2007

FEDERAL FINANCIAL INSTITUTIONS EXAMINATION COUNCIL
Balance Sheets

	As of December 31,	
	2006	2005
ASSETS		
CURRENT ASSETS		
Cash	$ 656,600	$ 598,259
Accounts receivable from member organizations (Note 3)	997,342	1,808,511
Other accounts receivable	243,181	557,347
Total current assets	1,897,123	2,964,117
CAPITAL ASSETS		
Furniture and equipment, at cost	56,121	60,446
Central Data Repository, at cost (Note 4)	12,905,335	12,055,244
Less accumulated depreciation	(2,947,171)	(629,743)
Net capital assets	10,014,285	11,485,947
Total assets	$ 11,911,408	$ 14,450,064
LIABILITIES AND CUMULATIVE RESULTS OF OPERATIONS		
CURRENT LIABILITIES		
Accounts payable and accrued liabilities payable to member organizations	$ 797,093	$ 1,099,400
Other accounts payable and accrued liabilities (Note 4)	645,438	1,482,102
Accrued payroll and annual leave	313,038	297,202
Deferred revenue (current portion) (Note 4)	2,355,548	2,277,189
Total current liabilities	4,111,117	5,155,893
LONG-TERM LIABILITIES		
Deferred revenue (non-current portion) (Note 4)	7,658,737	9,208,758
Deferred rent (Note 5)	58,164	75,604
Total long-term liabilities	7,716,901	9,284,362
Total liabilities	11,828,018	14,440,255
CUMULATIVE RESULTS OF OPERATIONS	83,390	9,809
Total liabilities and cumulative results of operations	$ 11,911,408	$ 14,450,064

See accompanying notes to financial statements.

FEDERAL FINANCIAL INSTITUTIONS EXAMINATION COUNCIL
Statements of Revenues and Expenses and Changes in Cumulative Results of Operations

	For the years ended December 31,	
	2006	2005
REVENUES		
Central Data Repository (Note 4)	$ 5,650,751	$ 3,205,813
Home Mortgage Disclosure Act (Note 6)	2,777,980	2,574,809
Tuition	2,066,960	1,991,263
Community Reinvestment Act	800,839	821,390
Uniform Bank Performance Report	595,781	524,350
Assessments on member organizations (Note 3)	548,800	419,055
Appraisal Subcommittee	189,397	183,566
Total revenues	12,630,508	9,720,246
EXPENSES		
Professional fees (Note 4)	4,041,444	3,241,435
Data processing	3,888,362	3,623,133
Depreciation (Note 4)	2,321,753	569,297
Salaries and related benefits	1,349,310	1,303,342
Rental of office space	469,860	437,564
Administration fees (Note 3)	183,000	175,000
Travel	98,582	116,098
Books and subscriptions	98,160	98,361
Rental and maintenance of office equipment	33,293	50,775
Printing	26,210	14,468
Office and other supplies	21,026	35,506
Other seminar expenses	11,801	71,285
Postage	10,571	17,195
Miscellaneous	3,555	1,294
Total expenses	12,556,927	9,754,753
RESULTS OF OPERATIONS	73,581	(34,507)
CUMULATIVE RESULTS OF OPERATIONS, Beginning of year	9,809	44,316
CUMULATIVE RESULTS OF OPERATIONS, End of year	$ 83,390	$ 9,809

See accompanying notes to financial statements.

FEDERAL FINANCIAL INSTITUTIONS EXAMINATION COUNCIL
Statements of Cash Flows

	For the years ended December 31,	
	2006	2005
CASH FLOWS FROM OPERATING ACTIVITIES		
RESULTS OF OPERATIONS	$ 73,581	$ (34,507)
Adjustments to reconcile results of operations to net cash provided by operating activities:		
Depreciation	2,321,753	569,297
(Increase) decrease in assets:		
Accounts receivable from member organizations	811,169	957,169
Other accounts receivable	314,166	(325,936)
Increase (decrease) in liabilities:		
Accounts payable and accrued liabilities to member organizations	(302,307)	348,351
Other accounts payable and accrued liabilities	(836,664)	(1,029,787)
Accrued payroll and annual leave	15,836	79,466
Deferred revenue (current and non-current)	(1,471,662)	2,402,187
Deferred rent	(17,440)	(4,441)
Net cash provided by operating activities	908,432	2,961,799
CASH FLOWS FROM INVESTING ACTIVITIES		
Capital expenditures (Note 4)	(850,091)	(2,971,484)
Net cash used in investing activities	(850,091)	(2,971,484)
NET INCREASE (DECREASE) IN CASH	58,341	(9,685)
CASH BALANCE, Beginning of year	598,259	607,944
CASH BALANCE, End of year	$ 656,600	$ 598,259

See accompanying notes to financial statements.

Notes to Financial Statements as of and for the Years Ended December 31, 2006 and 2005

(1) Organization and Purpose

The Federal Financial Institutions Examination Council (the "Council") was established under Title X of the Financial Institutions Regulatory and Interest Rate Control Act of 1978. The purpose of the Council is to prescribe uniform principles and standards for the federal examination of financial institutions and to make recommendations to promote uniformity in the supervision of these financial institutions. The five agencies which are represented on the Council, referred to hereinafter as member organizations, are as follows:

- Board of Governors of the Federal Reserve System (FRB)
- Federal Deposit Insurance Corporation (FDIC)
- National Credit Union Administration (NCUA)
- Office of the Comptroller of the Currency (OCC)
- Office of Thrift Supervision (OTS)

In accordance with the Financial Services Regulatory Relief Act of 2006, a representative state regulator was added as a full voting member of the FFIEC in October 2006.

The Council was given additional statutory responsibilities by section 340 of the Housing and Community Development Act of 1980, Public Law 96-399. Among these responsibilities are the implementation of a system to facilitate public access to data that depository institutions must disclose under the Home Mortgage Disclosure Act of 1975 (HMDA) and the aggregation of annual HMDA data, by census tract, for each metropolitan statistical area.

Appraisal Subcommittee—The Council's financial statements do not include financial data for the Appraisal Subcommittee. The Appraisal Subcommittee of the Council was created pursuant to Public Law 101-73, Title XI of the Financial Institutions Reform, Recovery, and Enforcement Act of 1989. The functions of the Appraisal Subcommittee are related to the certification and licensing of individuals who perform appraisals in connection with federally related real estate transactions. Members of the Appraisal Subcommittee consist of the designees of the heads of those agencies which comprise the Council and the designee of the head of the Department of Housing and Urban Development.

All functions and responsibilities assigned to the Council under Title XI are performed directly by the Appraisal Subcommittee without any need for approval or concurrence from the Council. The Appraisal Subcommittee has its own policies and procedures and submits its own Annual Report to the President of the Senate and Speaker of the House. The Council is not responsible for any debts incurred by the Subcommittee, nor are Subcommittee funds available for use by the Council.

(2) Significant Accounting Policies

The Council prepares its financial statements in accordance with accounting principles generally accepted in the United States of America based upon accounting standards issued by the Financial Accounting Standards Board (FASB).

The financial statements have been prepared on the accrual basis of accounting.

Revenues—Assessments made on member organizations for operating expenses and additions to property are based on expected cash needs. Amounts over- or under- assessed due to differences between actual and expected cash needs flow into "Cumulative Results of Operations" during the year and then are used to offset or increase the next year's assessment. Deficits in "Cumulative Results of Operations" can be made up in the following year's assessments.

Tuition revenue is adjusted at year-end so that total tuition revenue equals expenses incurred by the Examiner Education office. Any difference between revenue and expense is reported in accounts payable to member organizations if revenue exceeds expense, and in accounts receivable from member organizations if expenses exceed revenue.

Capital Assets—Furniture and equipment is recorded at cost less accumulated depreciation. Depreciation is calculated on a straight-line basis over the estimated useful lives of the assets, which range from four to ten years. Upon the sale or other disposition of a depreciable asset, the cost and related accumulated depreciation are removed from the accounts and any gain or loss is recognized. The Central Data Repository (CDR), a software project, is recorded at cost. (See Note 4)

Deferred Revenue—Deferred revenue represents cash collected and accounts receivable related to the CDR. (See Note 4)

Estimates—The preparation of financial statements in conformity with accounting principles generally accepted in the United States of America requires management to make estimates and assumptions that affect the reported amounts of assets and liabilities and the disclosure of contingent assets and liabilities at the date of the financial statements and the reported amounts of revenues and expenses during the reporting period. Actual results could differ from those estimates.

(3) Transactions with Member Organizations

	2006	2005
Accounts Receivable from Member Organizations		
Board of Governors of the Federal Reserve System	$ 169,562	$ 306,704
Federal Deposit Insurance Corporation	583,844	1,426,385
National Credit Union Administration	63,880	0
Office of the Comptroller of the Currency	111,909	58,160
Office of Thrift Supervision	68,147	17,262
	$ 997,342	$ 1,808,511

	2006	2005
The five member organizations are each assessed one-fifth of the expected cash needs based on the annual operating budget. The annual assessment for each member organization was:	$ 109,760	$ 83,811
The Council provides seminars in the Washington area and at regional locations throughout the country for member organization examiners and other agencies. The Council received tuition payments from member organizations in the amount of:	1,933,215	1,858,296
The FRB provided administrative support services to the Council at a cost of:	183,000	175,000
Member organizations provided office space, data processing related to Home Mortgage Disclosure Act (HMDA) and Community Reinvestment Act (CRA), and printing services to the Council. The Council paid member organizations:	3,674,682	3,809,989

The Council coordinates the production and distribution of the Uniform Bank Performance Reports (UBPR) through the FDIC. The Council is reimbursed for the direct cost of the operating expenses it incurs for this project.

The Council does not directly employ personnel but rather member organizations provide personnel to support Council Operations. These personnel are paid through the payroll systems of member organizations. Salaries and fringe benefits, including retirement benefit plan contributions, are reimbursed to these organizations. The Council does not have any post-retirement or post-employment benefit liabilities since Council personnel are included in the plans of the member organizations.

Member organizations are not reimbursed for the costs of personnel who serve as Council members and on the various task forces and committees of the Council. The value of these contributed services has not been included in the accompanying financial statements.

(4) Central Data Repository

In 2003, the Council entered into a ten year agreement with UNISYS, totaling approximately $40 million, to enhance the methods and systems used to collect, validate, process and distribute Call Report information, and to store this information in a Central Data Repository (CDR).

Notes continue on the following page.

The CDR was placed into production in October 2005. At that time, the Council began depreciating the CDR project on the straight-line basis over its estimated useful life of sixty-three months. The Council records depreciation expenses and recognizes the same amount of deferred revenue. The value of the CDR asset includes the fully accrued and paid cost.

	2006	2005
Capital Asset CDR		
Beginning balance	$11,955,244	$ 9,083,760
Capital expenditures	358,000	2,871,484
Software in use	12,313,244	11,955,244
Software in process	592,091	100,000
Total asset	$12,905,335	$12,055,244
Other Accounts Payable and Accrued Liabilities		
Payable to UNISYS for the CDR project	$ 576,443	$ 1,428,574
Other vendors unrelated to the CDR project	68,995	53,528
Total other accounts payable and accrued liabilities	$ 645,438	$ 1,482,102

Revenues-Central Data Repository—The Council is funding the project by billing the three participating Council member organizations (FRB, FDIC, and OCC) (See Note 2). The OCC's participation in cost sharing will not begin until the UBPR portion of the CDR becomes operational.

	2006	2005
Deferred revenue:		
Beginning balance	$11,485,947	$ 9,083,760
Additions	850,091	2,971,484
Less: Revenue recognized	(2,321,753)	(569,297)
Ending balance	$10,014,285	$11,485,947
Current portion deferred revenue	$ 2,355,548	$ 2,277,189
Long-term deferred revenue	7,658,737	9,208,758
	$10,014,285	$11,485,947
Total CDR revenue:		
Deferred revenue	$ 2,321,753	$ 569,297
Hosting and maintenance fees	3,328,998	2,636,516
Total CDR revenue	$ 5,650,751	$ 3,205,813

	2006	2005
Professional Fees		
Hosting and maintenance fees for the CDR project	$ 3,328,998	$ 2,636,516
Other professional fees unrelated to the CDR project	712,446	604,919
Total professional fees	$ 4,041,444	$ 3,241,435
Depreciation		
Depreciation for the CDR project	$ 2,321,753	$ 569,297
Other depreciation unrelated to the CDR project	0	0
Total depreciation	$ 2,321,753	$ 569,297
Average Monthly Amortization	$ 193,479	$ 189,766

(5) Deferred Rent

In 1998, the Council entered into a lease for office space at 2000 K Street, Washington, DC. This lease contains rent abatements and scheduled rent increases. In 2005, the Council entered into a lease for office and classroom space at an FDIC facility that contains scheduled rent increases over the term of the lease. In accordance with accounting principles generally accepted in the United States of America, rent abatements and scheduled rent increases must be considered in determining the annual rent expense to be recognized. The deferred rent represents the difference between the actual lease payments and the rent expense recognized.

(6) Other Revenue

	2006	2005
Home Mortgage Disclosure Act (HMDA)		
The Council recognized the following revenue from member organizations for the production and distribution of reports under the HMDA:	$ 1,880,259	$ 1,786,287
The Council recognized the following revenue from the Department of Housing and Urban Development's participation in the HMDA project:	589,547	503,004
The Council recognized the following revenue from the Mortgage Insurance Companies of America for performing HMDA related work:	287,481	258,257
The balance of the HMDA revenue for 2006 and 2005 was from sales to the public:	20,693	27,261
Total HMDA	$ 2,777,980	$ 2,574,809

Community Reinvestment Act (CRA)—The Council recognized revenue for support of operating expenses from the participating member agencies.

Uniform Bank Performance Report (UBPR)—The Council recognized revenue for coordinating and providing certain administrative support to the UBPR project.

Appraisal Subcommittee—The Council recognized revenue for providing space to the Appraisal Subcommittee.

(7) Operating Leases

The Council entered into operating leases to secure office and classroom space. Minimum future rental commitments under those operating leases having an initial or remaining noncancellable lease term in excess of one year at December 31, 2006, are as follows:

2007	$ 467,203
2008	417,980
2009	255,261
2010	0
2011	0
	$1,140,444

Rental expenses under these operating leases were $469,860 and $437,564 in 2006 and 2005, respectively.

KPMG LLP
2001 M Street, NW
Washington, DC 20036

Independent Auditors' Report on Internal Control over Financial Reporting

To the Federal Financial Institutions Examination Council:

We have audited the balance sheets of the Federal Financial Institutions Examination Council (the Council) as of December 31, 2006 and 2005, and the related statements of revenues and expenses and changes in cumulative results of operations, and cash flows (hereinafter referred to as "financial statements") for the years then ended, and have issued our report thereon dated March 7, 2007.

We conducted our audits in accordance with auditing standards generally accepted in the United States of America and the standards applicable to financial audits contained in *Government Auditing Standards*, issued by the Comptroller General of the United States. Those standards require that we plan and perform the audits to obtain reasonable assurance about whether the financial statements are free of material misstatement.

INTERNAL CONTROL OVER FINANCIAL REPORTING

The management of the Council is responsible for establishing and maintaining effective internal control. In planning and performing our 2006 audit, we considered the Council's internal control over financial reporting as a basis for designing our auditing procedures for the purpose of expressing our opinion on the financial statements. We limited our internal control testing to those controls necessary to achieve the objectives described in *Government Auditing Standards*. The objective of our audit was not to express an opinion on the effectiveness of the Council's internal control over financial reporting. Accordingly, we do not express an opinion on the effectiveness of the Council's internal control over financial reporting.

A control deficiency exists when the design or operation of a control does not allow management or employees, in the normal course of performing their assigned functions, to prevent or detect misstatements on a timely basis. A significant deficiency is a control deficiency, or combination of control deficiencies, that adversely affects the Council's ability to initiate, authorize, record, process, or report financial data reliably in accordance with generally accepted accounting principles such that there is more than a remote likelihood that a misstatement of the Council's financial statements that is more than inconsequential will not be prevented or detected by the entity's internal control.

A material weakness is a significant deficiency, or combination of significant deficiencies, that results in more than a remote likelihood that a material misstatement of the financial statements will not be prevented or detected by the Council's internal control.

Our consideration of internal control over financial reporting was for the limited purpose described in the first paragraph of this section and would not necessarily identify all deficiencies in internal control that might be significant deficiencies or material weaknesses. We did not identify any deficiencies in internal control over financial reporting that we consider to be material weaknesses, as defined above.

We noted certain matters that we reported to the management of the Council in a separate letter dated March 7, 2007.

This report is intended solely for the information and use of the Council's management, the Office of Inspector General of the Board of Governors of the Federal Reserve System, the U.S. Government Accountability Office, and the U.S. Congress and is not intended to be and should not be used by anyone other than these specified parties.

KPMG LLP

March 7, 2007

KPMG LLP
2001 M Street, NW
Washington, DC 20036

Independent Auditors' Report on Compliance and Other Matters

To the Federal Financial Institutions Examination Council:

We have audited the balance sheets of the Federal Financial Institutions Examination Council (the Council) as of December 31, 2006 and 2005, and the related statements of revenues and expenses and changes in cumulative results of operations, and cash flows (hereinafter referred to as "financial statements") for the years then ended, and have issued our report thereon dated March 7, 2007.

We conducted our audits in accordance with auditing standards generally accepted in the United States of America and the standards applicable to financial audits contained in *Government Auditing Standards*, issued by the Comptroller General of the United States. Those standards require that we plan and perform the audit to obtain reasonable assurance about whether the financial statements are free of material misstatement.

The management of the Council is responsible for complying with laws, regulations, and contracts applicable to the Council. As part of obtaining reasonable assurance about whether the Council's financial statements are free of material misstatement, we performed tests of the Council's compliance with certain provisions of laws, regulations, and contracts, noncompliance with which could have a direct and material effect on the determination of the financial statement amounts. We limited our tests of compliance to the provisions described in the preceding sentence, and we did not test compliance with all laws, regulations, and contracts applicable to the Council. However, providing an opinion on compliance with those provisions was not an objective of our audit, and accordingly, we do not express such an opinion.

The results of our tests of compliance described in the preceding paragraph, disclosed no instances of noncompliance or other matters that are required to be reported under *Government Auditing Standards*.

This report is intended solely for the information and use of the Council's management, the Office of Inspector General of the Board of Governors of the Federal Reserve System, the U.S. Government Accountability Office, and the U.S. Congress and is not intended to be and should not be used by anyone other than these specified parties.

KPMG LLP

March 7, 2007

Appendix C: Maps of Agency Regions and Districts

38 Board of Governors of the Federal Reserve System
39 Federal Deposit Insurance Corporation
40 National Credit Union Administration
41 Office of the Comptroller of the Currency
42 Office of Thrift Supervision

The Federal Reserve System Districts

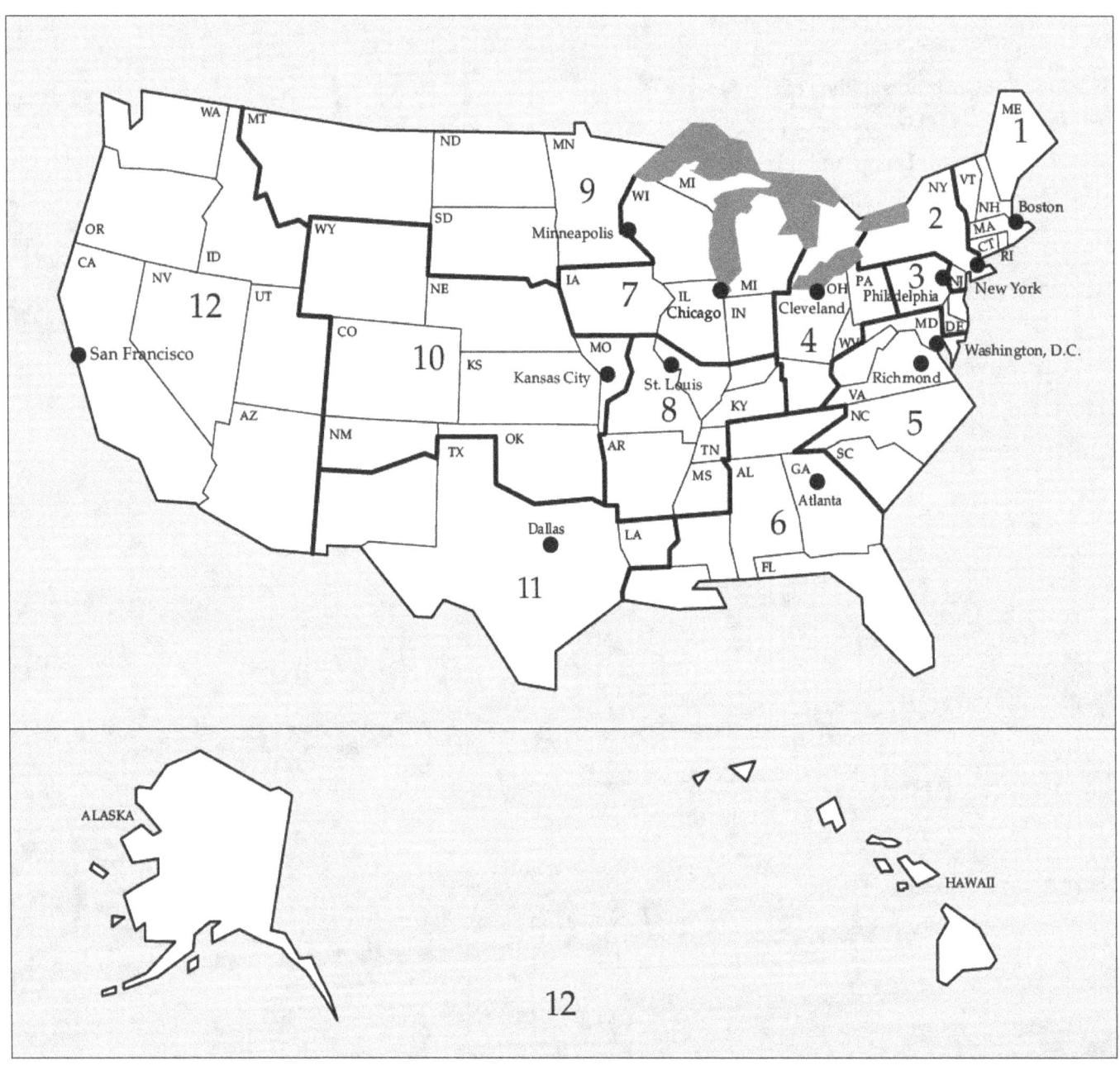

Federal Deposit Insurance Corporation Regions
(Supervision and Compliance)

* Two area offices are located in Boston (reports to New York) and Memphis (reports to Dallas)

NATIONAL CREDIT UNION ADMINISTRATION

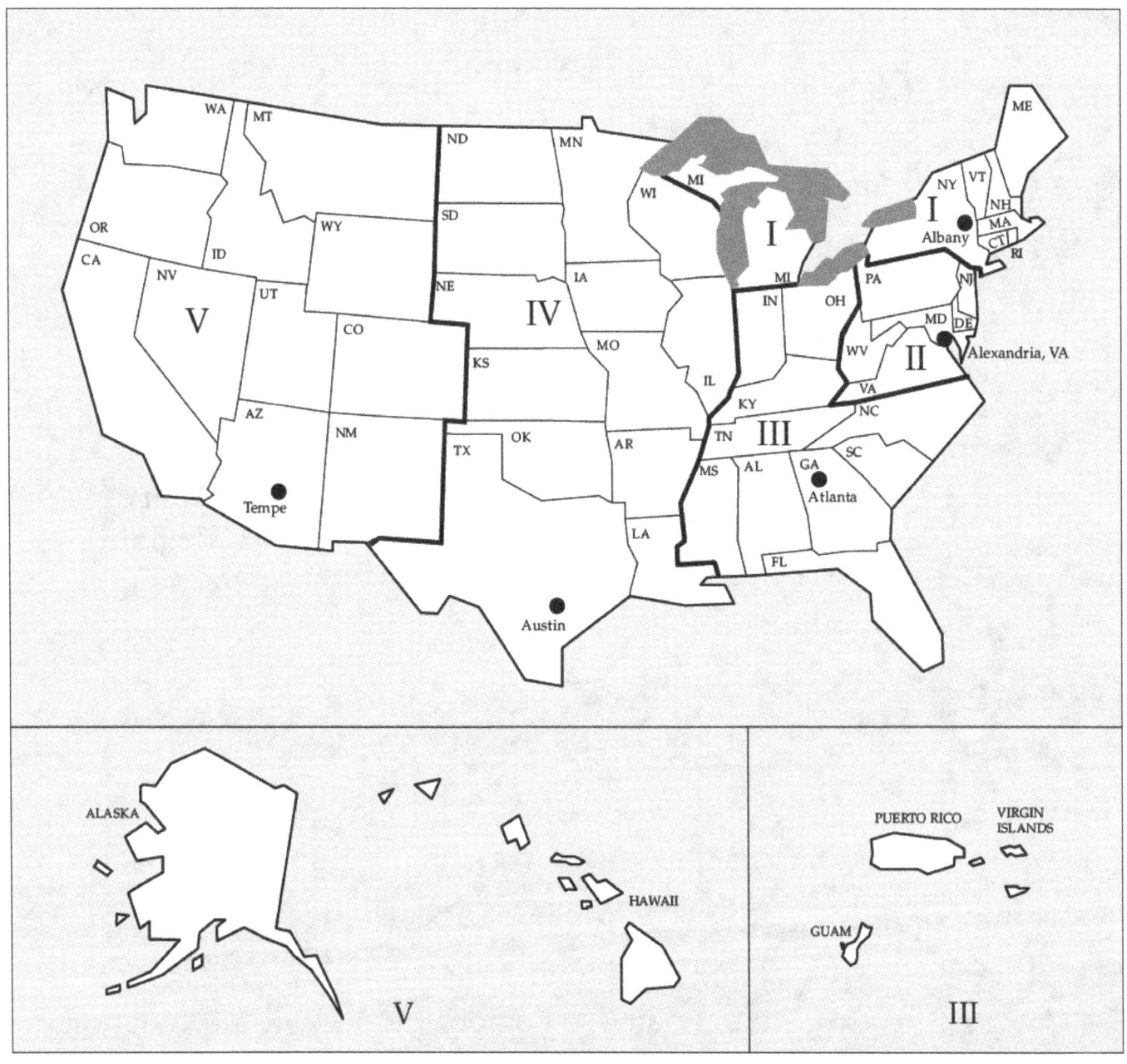

COMPTROLLER OF THE CURRENCY DISTRICT ORGANIZATION

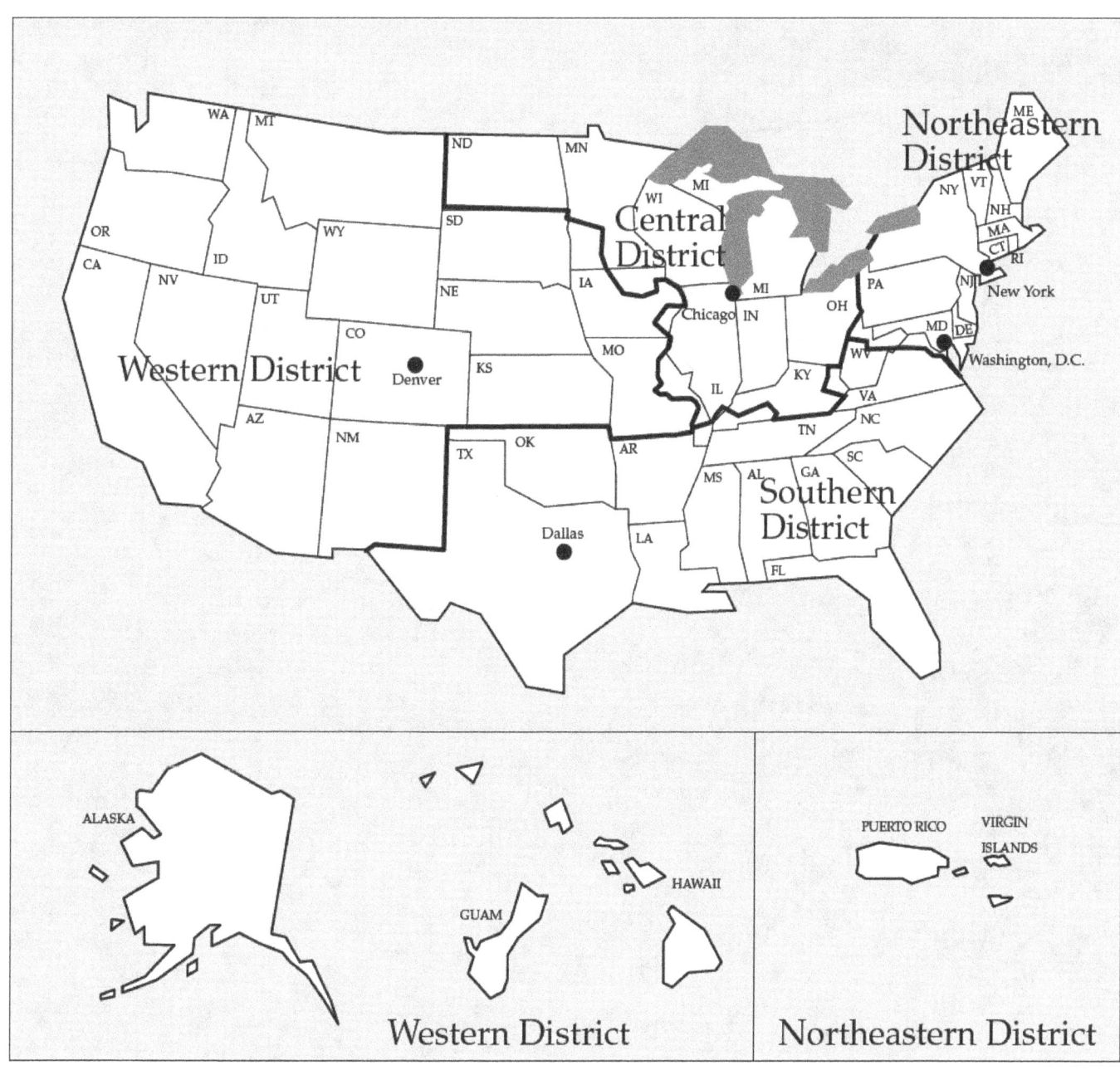

Office of Thrift Supervision

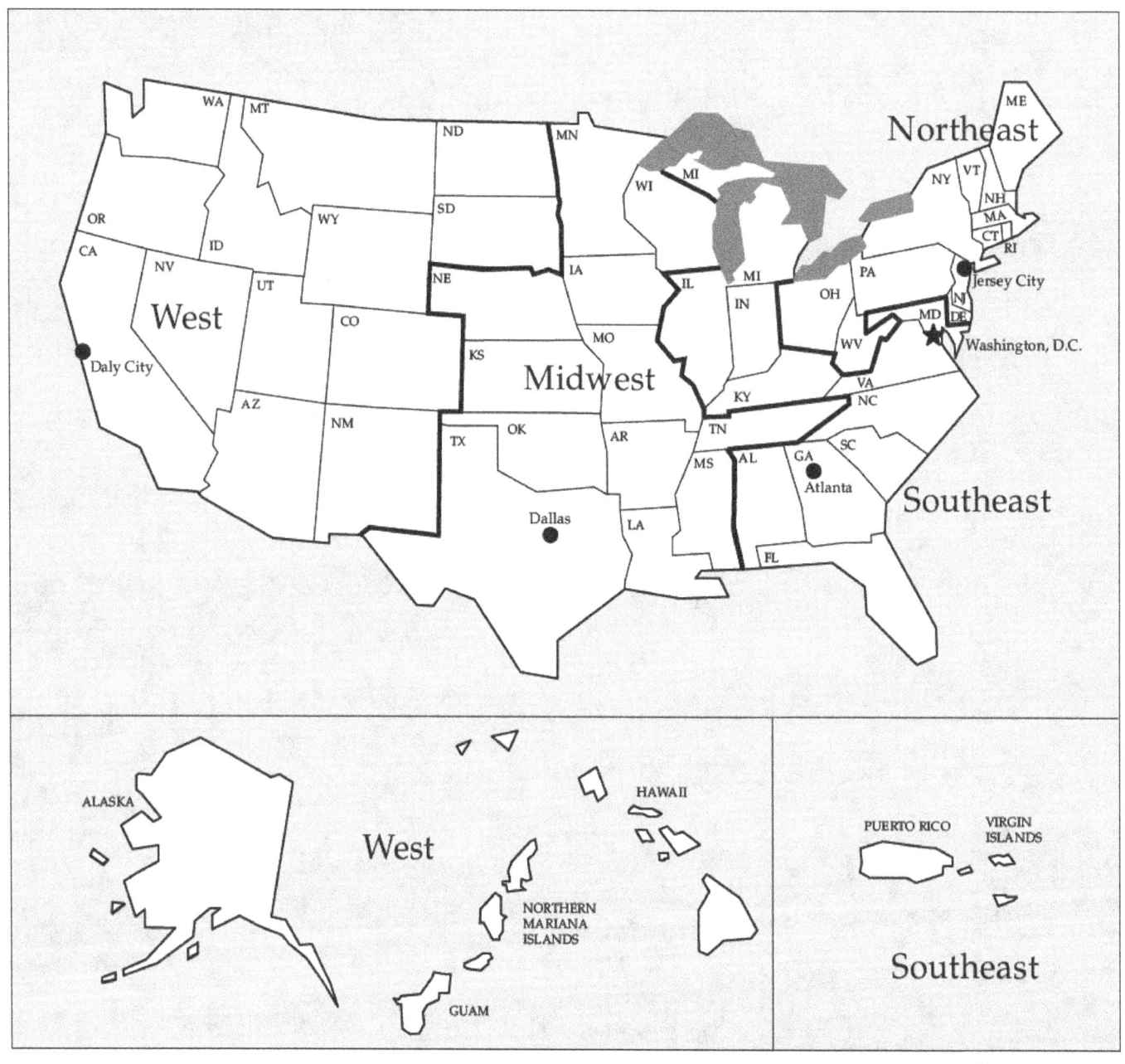

APPENDIX D: ORGANIZATIONAL LISTING OF PERSONNEL

Organization, December 31, 2006

Members of the Council

John C. Dugan, *Chairman*
 Comptroller
 Office of the Comptroller of the Currency (OCC)

Susan Schmidt Bies, *Vice Chairman*
 Member
 Board of Governors of the Federal Reserve System (FRB)

Steven L. Antonakes,
 State Liaison Committee Representative
 Commissioner of Banks
 Boston, MA

Sheila C. Bair
 Chairman
 Federal Deposit Insurance Corporation (FDIC)

JoAnn Johnson
 Chairman
 National Credit Union Administration (NCUA)

John M. Reich
 Director
 Office of Thrift Supervision (OTS)

State Liaison Committee (SLC)

Steven L. Antonakes, *Chairman*
 Commissioner of Banks
 Boston, MA

Jerrie J. Lattimore
 Administrator,
 North Carolina
 Credit Union Division

D. Eric McClure
 Commissioner
 Missouri Division of Finance

Jonathan Smith
 Review Examiner
 Delaware State Banking Department

Mick Thompson
 Commissioner,
 Oklahoma State Banking Department

Council Staff Officers

Tamara J. Wiseman
Executive Secretary

Interagency Staff Groups

Agency Liaison Group

Roger T. Cole (FRB)
George French (FDIC)
David M. Marquis (NCUA)
Scott M. Polakoff (OTS)
Emory Wayne Rushton (OCC)

Legal Advisory Group

Julie L. Williams, *Chairperson* (OCC)
Scott Alvarez (FRB)
John Bowman (OTS)
Robert M. Fenner (NCUA)
Douglas Jones (FDIC)

Task Force on Consumer Compliance

Ann Jaedicke, *Chairperson* (OCC)
Matthew Biliouris (NCUA)
Glenn Loney (FRB)
Robert W. Mooney (FDIC)
Montrice G. Yakimov (OTS)

Task Force on Examiner Education

Betty J. Rudolph, *Chairperson* (FDIC)
Matthew Amato (OTS)
Cheryl Davis (OCC)
Joy Lee (NCUA)
William G. Spaniel (FRB)

Task Force on Information Sharing

Robin Stefan, *Chairman* (OCC)
Roger Blake (NCUA)
Michael Kraemer (FRB)
Karl Krichbaum (FDIC)
Pamela Schaar (OTS)

Task Force on Reports

Robert F. Storch, *Chairman* (FDIC)
Zane D. Blackburn (OCC)
James Caton (OTS)
Charles Holm (FRB)
Debra Tobin (NCUA)

Task Force on Supervision

Roger T. Cole, *Chairman* (FRB)
Scott Albinson (OTS)
Joy Lee (NCUA)
Emory Wayne Rushton (OCC)
Sandra Thompson (FDIC)

Task Force on Surveillance Systems

Robin Stefan, *Chairman* (OCC)
James Caton (OTS)
Mat Mattson (FRB)
Michael Ryan (NCUA)
Scott Patterson (FDIC)